Breaking Compromises

Breaking Compromises

Opportunities for Action in Consumer Markets from the Boston Consulting Group

Edited by Michael J. Silverstein and George Stalk, Jr.

John Wiley & Sons, Inc.

New York ♦ Chichester ♦ Weinheim ♦ Brisbane ♦ Singapore ♦ Toronto

Copyright © 2000 by The Boston Consulting Group, Inc. All rights reserved.
Published by John Wiley & Sons, Inc.
Published simultaneously in Canada.

This publication is designed to provide accurate and authoritative information in regard to
the subject matter covered. It is sold with the understanding that the publisher is not
engaged in rendering professional services. If legal, accounting, medical, psychological or
any other expert assistance is required, the services of a competent professional person
should be sought.

ISBN 0-471-38433-X

Printed in the United States of America

10 9 8 7 6 5 4 3 2 1

v

Contents

Preface

Every day we hear, "*It* can't be done. We tried that and *it* didn't work. Our senior management won't permit *it*."

"*It*" is a new idea or a new way of going to market. *It* often requires behavioral change and investment. *It* always requires risk taking and initiative. The discouraging response is rarely based on facts, market testing, or even a fair and open discussion.

The Boston Consulting Group's quest is to change both the response and the result. Our belief is that the combination of analysis, dialogue, and courage can create breakthrough results. It takes all three to stay ahead of constant change, understand the consumer's point of view, break the seemingly intractable compromises we all unthinkingly accept, and create an adaptive and responsive organization.

Breakthroughs are tough. One of our clients, a genius who has invented a series of retail blockbusters, calls it "seeing around the corner and creating 'next.' " To create a successful "next," you have to focus on the consumer's total experience with your brand, as well as on his or her hopes and dreams. Your goal is to develop products that fulfill needs customers weren't even aware of.

Whether it's a snack, a washing machine, a frozen dinner, or a specialty retail store, the brand experience begins the moment the consumer learns about the brand and continues through repurchase after repurchase. It includes everything from store location and decor to package design, mechandising, product quality, credit policies, staff and management cultures, after-sales services, and even parking. For any targeted group of consumers, however, some elements will be more important than others; and for any business, some will be more cost effective to undertake. Therefore, a business doesn't need to do *everything* right as long as it does the *right* things right—for the target consumer.

Doing the right things right begins with *mapping* the consumer's total experience with the brand, discovering the reasons for defection, and plotting the opportunities for intervention. But since a company can't improve everything, it has to *measure* the size of the prize—for both consumers and the business. Once it knows what to do, it can *create* a design plan that includes all the right tools and then roll it out to the whole business system to *capture* new apostles for the brand.

It's not surprising to hear the same names over and over again when people talk about their favoite brands: Fritos, Big Mac, Lexus, Nordstrom, Victoria's Secret, Sony, Absolut, KitchenAid, DisneyWorld, Pokémon, Windex, and Ford's F150 light truck. The companies that own those brands go out of their way to forge lifetime bonds with their customers. They know which tradeoffs they need to make in order to provide the kind of experiences their customers will talk about. Their passion for their customers and their belief in thorough research over guesswork ensure that they will do the right things for their businesses as well as for their customers.

Most ordinary mortals settle for extrapolating from current trends. But if you want to create the future rather than play catch-up, you need to ask yourself some tough questions, such as:

- What is our brand's most serious failing?

- What latent dissatisfactions are we overlooking?

- Is our organization committed to finding a better way?

- How good are our best ideas and how long will they last?

- How much change can we learn to sustain and how quickly can we do it?

The answers to these questions will come from fresh ways of looking at consumers, your competitors, and your businesses. For the past few years, we have published a series of articles called Opportunities for Action in Consumer Markets. Our themes are insight, initiative, and innovation. The articles explore how leading companies find ideas, identify the best of them, bring together resources to test and learn from the ideas, and, ultimately, make them work. The articles cover the major forces driving consumer and retail businesses over the past half decade, including globalization, electronic commerce, brand renaissance, pricing, database marketing, and value-chain deconstruction.

We are offering this selection from our series because we want you to achieve a new level of aspiration, courage, and intensity. We hope you'll find at least one or two articles that speak to the issues you've been struggling with. We also hope you'll share the ideas that come to your mind as you read this anthology.

Michael J. Silverstein

George Stalk, Jr.

Michael J. Silverstein is a senior vice president in the Chicago office of The Boston Consulting Group and head of the firm's global Consumer and Retail practice. He can be reached at silverstein.michael@bcg.com or 312-993-3306. George Stalk, Jr., is a senior vice president in BCG's Toronto office. He can be reached at stalk.george@bcg.com.

Acknowledgments

This book is the product of many years of collective experience helping consumer companies find productive and original ways to meet the challenges of their businesses. We want to thank our clients for the opportunity to serve them and for the lessons we have learned with them. They are the inspiration for our insights. Of course, many friends and colleagues at BCG have also contributed to our success.

Of particular importance are the core members of the firm's Consumer and Retail practice. They are the holders of our mantra—focus, collaborate, invent.

René Abate, Harri Andersson, Jim Andrew, Rob Archacki, Allison Bailey, Brad Banducci, Felix Barber, Tommaso Barracco, Anne Beall, Jorge Becerra, Joël Ben-zimra, Rohit Bhagat, Paolo Biancardi, Eric Bismuth, Marc Bitzer, Rolf Bixner, Jill Black, Marcus Bökkerink, Tracey Breazeale, Willie Burnside, Charmian Caines, Andrew Cainey, Giovanni Castellucci, Mark Chapman, Jacques Chapuis, Thierry Chassaing, Raffaele Cicala, Jennifer Comparoni, Carlos Costa, Joe Davis, Joan Dea, Mike Deimler, Patrick Ducasse, David Edelman, Brian Elliott, Philip Evans, Jeannine Everett, Ahmed Fahour, Paul Fenaroli, Neil Fiske, Michel Frédeau, Mark Freedman, Grant Freeland, Marin Gjaja, Emile Gostelie, Larry Green, Michael Grindfors, Steve Gunby, Wahid Hamid, Katrina Helmkamp, Jim Hemerling, Dieter Heuskel, K2 Hori, Tom Hout, Hubert Hsu, Barbara Hulit, Jon Isaacs, Alan Jackson, Mark Joiner, Barry Jones, Lidia Juszko, Nicolas Kachaner, Takashi Kaneko, Nicholas Keuper, Mia Kirchgaessner, Noboru Kotani, Matt Krentz, Beth Kressley, Rob Lachenauer, David Lack, Kirsten Lange, Sara LaPorta, Pete Lawyer, Rich Lesser, Tomas Linden, John Lindquist, Alex Lintner, Roland Loehner, Tom Lutz, D.G. MacPherson, Joe Manget, Jim Maritan, Heino Meerkatt, Antonella Mei-Pochtler, José Manuel Méndez, Takashi Mitachi, Neil Monnery, Sandy Moose, Yves Morieux, Atsushi Morisawa, Dean Nelson, Mirko Nikolic, Petter Norstrand, Scott Ohman, Paul Orlander, Joachim Palme, George Pappas, David Pecaut, Stephanie Peponis, Marc Pfitzer, Molly Pieroni, Filip Pintelon, Nevada Powe, Anthony Pralle, Stefan Rasch, Byung-Nam Rhee, Martina Rissmann, Raúl Rivera, Ruben Rodriguez, Alison Sander, Olivier Scaramucci, Maria Schaecher, Jan Scheffler, Wouter-Jan Schouten, Paul Shepanski, Larry Shulman, Hal Sirkin, Luca Solca, George Stalk, Peter Stanger, Scott Stephenson, Karen Sterling, Greg Sutherland, Miki Tsusaka, Henry Vogel, Archibald von Keyserlingk, Carina von Knoop, Rashid Wasti, Tigre Wenrich, Michael Westhoven, Peter Wetenhall, Anne Wilkins, Sarah Wilshaw-Sparkes,

Wendi Wolf-Lewitt, John Wong, Tom Wurster, Dave Young, and Carla Zolin-Meyer.

In addition, we want to acknowledge our editing champions, Sally Seymour and Sharon Slodki. Sally is the tireless behind-the-scenes discussion partner, editorial artist, and contributor for the series. Sharon attempts to ensure that we are in line with the laws of good communication. We thank them both for their efforts, but any lapses in content are our own. And a special thanks to Janet Emmons, our marketing operations manager. She took charge of the overall design of the book and managed its production.

We also want to thank Marge Branecki and Emmanuel Huet, the Consumer and Retail practice assistants. They keep us informed, organized, and functioning seamlessly.

Finally, we must express our deepest appreciation to John Clarkeson, chairman of the board, and Carl Stern, president and CEO. Good friends and valued colleagues, they remind us every day that insight, impact, and trust are what give BCG its soul and bind us together.

Michael J. Silverstein

BREAKING COMPROMISES

George Stalk, Jr., David Pecaut, and Benjamin Burnett

Many companies today are searching for growth. How and where should they look? One powerful way to grow is through innovations that break the  fundamental "compromises" of a business. When a company successfully breaks a compromise, it releases enormous trapped value. Breakaway growth can be the result.

Compromises are concessions demanded of consumers by most companies in an industry. They occur when the industry imposes its own operating constraints on customers. Usually, customers accept those compromises as just the way the business works—inevitable tradeoffs that have to be endured.

But a compromise is different from a tradeoff. In choosing a hotel room, for instance, a customer can *trade off* luxury for economy by choosing between a Ritz-Carlton and a Best Western. Until recently, however, most hotels forced all customers to compromise by not permitting check-in before 4:00 p.m. No law of nature or economics decrees that hotel rooms can't be ready before late afternoon.

Uncompromising Opportunity

The idea of compromises can be a useful organizing principle to focus an entire company on growth. It provides a systematic way to search for growth opportunities that are logical extensions of a company's existing business system.

Take the example of Circuit City's recent foray into the used-car business through the creation of a network of used-car superstores under the brand name CarMax. Annual used-car sales in North America top $200 billion, making it the third-largest consumer-spending category, behind food and clothing. What's more, few experiences are more fraught with compromises. Shopping for a used car is extremely time-consuming. And the buyer is at a fundamental disadvantage, ignorant about the actual condition of the product and subject to high-pressure sales tactics.

Circuit City concluded that many of the distinguishing capabilities of its consumer electronics business could be used to break the compromises imposed on used-car buyers. Circuit City is known for the wide variety of its merchandise. CarMax takes the same approach. The typical used-car dealer has only 30 vehicles in stock; CarMax sites have up to 1,500. That makes it easy for customers to compare makes and styles. CarMax further enhances choice and lowers search costs by harnessing Circuit City's considerable expertise in information systems. At CarMax, customers have access to easy-to-use computer kiosks that allow them to review the inventory of available cars at all CarMax stores in the region.

CarMax hasn't hesitated to deviate from the Circuit City model when the strategic logic requires it. For instance, Circuit City pays percentage-of-sales commissions to its consumer electronics sales force, but CarMax does not. Because a major compromise in used cars is pressure selling, the unit has developed a compensation system that encourages no-haggle pricing and no-hassle guarantees. The result: an integrated business system that offers a fundamentally different experience to used-car buyers, and a business model that has allowed CarMax to capture roughly 15 points of share in the markets where it is active.

A Pathway to Growth

Compromises are inherent in any business. Even when a company breaks one compromise, it usually ends up creating another. By focusing on compromises, a company can continuously uncover fresh opportunities and thus sustain growth over time.

The financial services company Charles Schwab, for example, was founded on the breaking of a compromise. The company began as a discount brokerage in 1975, when the deregulation of U.S. security markets made it unnecessary for individual investors to pay high fees to full-service brokers.

But Schwab didn't stop there. Next, it broke the compromise set up by the discount brokerage houses themselves. Although these new firms offered low prices, most of them also provided unreliable service. By investing in computer technology that allowed almost immediate confirmation of orders over the telephone, Schwab could combine low prices with levels of responsiveness unusual in its industry. Subsequently, Schwab added convenience, flexibility, and ease of transferring funds to its value proposition by offering 24-hour-a-day, seven-day-a-week service, the Schwab One cash-management account, and automated phone and electronic trading.

Recently, Schwab has used its compromise-breaking capabilities to enter the mutual fund business. Most people invest in several fund families to achieve diversification. But diversification often comes at the price of frustration. It means dealing with a confusing variety of statements, rules, and sales representatives. In 1992, Schwab introduced OneSource—a single point of purchase for more than 350 no-load mutual funds. In the more than 20 years since its founding, Schwab has evolved from a simple discount broker to a comprehensive self-help financial supermarket and has generated an annual growth rate of 20 to 25 percent.

Creativity, Flexibility, and Nerve

For a company to grow by breaking compromises, it must have the creativity to translate customer dissatisfactions into new value propositions, the flexibility to engage in constant reorientation of its business system, and the nerve to challenge business-as-usual in its industry. There are three basic steps:

Get inside the customer experience. Start by asking your managers and employees to immerse themselves in the customer's experience. It is critical to develop a visceral feel for the compromises that consumers encounter when they do business with you.

A compromise often becomes visible when consumers have to modify their behavior to use a company's product or service. So pay special attention to the compensatory behaviors that customers engage in to get around the constraints your product or service imposes on them. In the brokerage business, for instance, it was common knowledge that customers often called back a second or even a third time to confirm that their trade had gone through at the price requested. By paying careful attention to this behavior, Schwab realized that the ability to provide immediate confirmation when an order was taken would eliminate the extra calls, saving customers a lot of trouble and giving Schwab a significant advantage over its competitors.

Travel up the hierarchy of compromises. Once the organization is focused on the customer experience, learn to recognize three different types of compromises, each with increasing potential to create value.

Some of the most obvious can be found in your company's existing products or services. It was Chrysler's awareness of the compromises between station wagons (based on a car platform) and vans (based on a truck platform) that led to the minivan, a van based on a car platform. In the ten years after Chrysler introduced the minivan in 1984, minivan sales grew eight times as fast as industry sales overall.

Other, more powerful compromises can be found at the level of an entire product category. Witness how Nike has transformed the athletic footwear category by combining continuous innovation in shoe design with the proliferation of narrowly defined customer segments. Nike doesn't just make basketball shoes. It makes "Air Jordans," "Force," and "Flight," each designed for a different playing style—with different design requirements— and a different image.

The most powerful compromises are often the hardest to identify: broad social dissatisfactions that may have little to do with your product or industry but a lot to do with how your customers live their lives. For example, long-term social and economic trends are causing more and more people to manage their own investments. And yet, lack of time and growing economic complexity can make this an immensely frustrating task. Schwab's ability to address that frustration is a big factor in its success.

Reconstruct your value chain. Defining new value propositions for the customer is necessary but not sufficient. You must also use the compromises you break to redefine the competitive dynamics of your industry, to ensure that the economic value liberated by compromise breaking flows to you rather than to your competitors.

So think of compromises as an opportunity to reshape the value chain of your industry to your advantage. When Schwab entered the mutual fund business, its first thought was to create its own family of funds. Careful analysis of the industry value chain, however, revealed an even bigger opportunity: to become an intermediary between its own customer base and a large number of subscale mutual-fund companies. Through OneSource, the firm serves the needs of the fund companies by providing them with economies of scale they could not achieve on their own. At the same time, Schwab interposes itself between the funds and the customer. Schwab's ownership of the direct customer relationship now provides a platform for growth in other financial services, such as insurance.

To break compromises, executives must first break with the conventional wisdom of their industry—about customers, about industry practices, and about the economics of the business. When they do, faster growth and improved profitability are the result.

This article was first published in May 1997.

Part One

OPERATING EFFICIENCY

David C. Edelman and Jeff Levitan

More than half of the CEOs responding to a recent *Bozell Worldwide/ Fortune Magazine* poll claimed they were responsible for managing their brands.  Yet only two companies, Coca-Cola and McDonald's, were rated by a majority of the same CEOs as effective brand managers. Do CEOs lack brand management skills or are they really not in charge of their brands? The answer is a little of both.

The problem starts with how companies define brand management and groom brand managers. A recent Boston Consulting Group review of the brand management practices of a variety of consumer marketers indicates that most companies still see brand management as advertising, promotions, and new product launches. Few companies explicitly define the brand management process, and even fewer have programs for developing managers with skills broad enough to manage a brand.

The CEO's brand management role in most companies consists mainly of copy approval, pricing strategy, and timing. Those closest to the brand on a day-to-day basis are usually junior managers who have had a series of 18-month stints in a limited set of categories. These managers have had little experience managing a full profit-and-loss statement; have rarely worked outside the marketing organization (in manufacturing or sales, for instance); are focusing on the short term, with few incentives to consider investments for a longer-term payoff; and often don't understand what the brand stands for in the consumer's mind.

Today's brand managers need new skills because they must now play two different and increasingly complicated roles: marketing specialist and orchestrator. As *marketing specialists,* they must cope with an explosion of data and a need for highly targeted and complex marketing strategies. As *orchestrators,* they face ever more elaborate and geographically dispersed company structures, which make strategies increasingly difficult to execute.

Reengineering Isn't Enough

Recognizing these changes, companies all over the world are reorganizing and reengineering. But as helpful as those efforts may be, no lasting solution is possible without attention to the skills of the marketing line management.

Gillette learned this lesson in the late 1980s, when it initiated an aggressive global strategy for its core shaving products. It divested nonperforming assets, withdrew support from nonstrategic businesses, realigned marketing teams, created a group responsible for global strategy, and redefined the local organization's role. Gillette also reengineered many core marketing processes, including planning and new product development. But results didn't begin to show until the company acquired new resources, defined new roles, and imparted the new skills necessary to manage a global brand.

Acquiring the Right Resources

To acquire the capabilities they need, companies can either hire outsiders or train their own people. Many companies, such as IBM, General Motors, AT&T, and Microsoft, are raiding the ranks of packaged goods marketers to find new brand-management leaders. This can be an efficient short-term option, but there are risks: even if the organization doesn't reject a transplanted manager, few companies consciously spell out how they will draw on their new blood to build a broader range of skilled managers. Training internal candidates boosts morale, retains organizational knowledge, and contributes to a stable culture. But internal development can be difficult if there's no road map to guide the process or if time is tight.

To succeed today, companies need an aggressive, explicit skill-development strategy that combines internal training with external hiring to build a pool of talent with general management skills. Most companies already participate in some form of skill development, but only a few have a *comprehensive*, highly visible program that will put them ahead of the competition. Such a program clearly defines the skills required over the next few years, matches skills to jobs, accounts for how skill needs might change with geographic regions and time, and provides an explicit method for tracking and rewarding employees' progress.

Developing Organizational Resources

Choosing the right program means understanding the levers for effective brand management in your line of business, comparing them with what you have now, and thinking about how to bridge the gaps. In our experience, the companies that have been most successful at developing a pipeline of capable brand managers have done so in three steps:

1. Define a skill development pathway for different career levels. Many organizations have lost sight of what it takes to be a successful brand manager today. The skills that managers need span a broad range of technical, communications, and analytic capabilities, including

- reinventing a category to address latent consumer needs

- mobilizing a cross-functional set of managers to deliver new products and services

- mastering an increasingly complex array of marketing and distribution channels to reach customers

- using information technology to establish and manage individual customer relationships

Besides formal training programs, consumer marketers such as Colgate-Palmolive and Kao are experimenting with a variety of ways to help employees develop and demonstrate new skills. These include

- identifying divisions to act as centers of excellence for training untested managers under the guidance of seasoned managers

- defining a balanced job-rotation path to ensure that managers have a full set of business experiences

- basing promotion on skill development to make managers more responsible for setting their own development agendas

- tying bonuses to continuing performance in a former division in order to encourage managers to take a longer-term view of their decisions

It won't be easy to build a program around these skills, but doing so ensures that employees will be able to focus their efforts in the right direction. The initiative should begin with putting skill development on the table as an explicit part of the senior management agenda. At a leading U.S. beverage company, for example, the top executives recently met for several days to develop full descriptions of the skills they needed for marketing. That was the first time senior executives consciously addressed skills as a core part of company strategy, and it didn't go unnoticed in the organization. The executives are now communicating their criteria to employees, who feel supported rather than threatened by the new demands.

2. Assess and track employee performance. Once the required skills have been identified, a process for monitoring skill development needs to be created. A centralized database will help, but it should do more than simply collect data. It must provide a clear definition of the skills needed, match them with jobs and geographic locations, and track and evaluate employee progress. In addition, it should provide ready access to information on changes in skill requirements.

Danone, the European yogurt maker, adopted elements of this approach in its resource development program. After defining the marketing skills needed, it helped managers acquire them with a promotion path that required "credits" in multiple functions to progress up the career ladder. By offering salary increases faster than job promotions, the company helped managers adapt to the more rigorous climb up the career ladder.

3. Continually assess the required skills against the available talent. Rather than delegate reviews of skill requirements to the human resources department, senior management should make skill development a permanent part of the annual strategic-planning process. To this end, line managers need to be explicit about what new skills are needed, where they see gaps, and how they plan to develop their key people.

Many consumer-marketing companies have initiated broad reengineering programs for brand management. But the CEOs of those companies will continue to rate one another as having poorly managed brands until they directly address the skill development of their brand managers.

This article was first published in January 1996.

Neil S. Fiske

Leading consumer marketers have mastered an intricate set of skills that deliver fresher products at lower costs, with dramatically less inventory and

fewer fixed assets. This capability has become an advantage that boosts sales, share, and profit. Because it happens inside the company, it's primarily a hidden advantage. Competitors don't realize they've been outdistanced until it's too late to catch up.

If you haven't cut your finished-goods inventory in half or more while delivering 99.9 percent filled orders, then perhaps the supply-chain revolution is leaving you behind.

For one food company, the mantra is "Make in a week what you sell in a week." The idea is to synchronize production with consumer demand weekly, significantly cutting inventory, logistics costs, and time to market.

In the past, this company had manufactured for long-run-length efficiency four to six weeks in advance of demand. The result: 45 days of inventory, large fixed investments in physical storage, high reclamations, multiple handlings, and poor product quality. Today its supply chain is working toward 10 days of inventory—3 for the production cycle, another 3 for transportation, and 4 for system safety stock—or a reduction of more than 70 percent.

Most companies, however, have failed to make such dramatic progress. Packaged goods companies and grocery retailers have been talking for five years about efficient consumer response programs, yet inventory days for manufacturers and retailers alike have remained remarkably stable. (See Exhibit 1.)

Well-intentioned companies fall short because they define supply-chain improvement too narrowly, look only for first-order benefits, lack consistent CEO leadership, or try to do too much too fast. To succeed, you need a common framework, breakthrough redesign, and seamless execution supported by everyone from those on the shop floor to those in the executive suite. We recommend a three-step process to get there.

Step 1. Understand where profits are being lost.

Before you can change any system, you have to know why it operates as it currently does. This sounds obvious, but few companies appreciate just how deeply they have to go to satisfy this requirement. It means *quantifying each day of inventory and lost time, every dollar of cost and lost profit.*

Exhibit 1

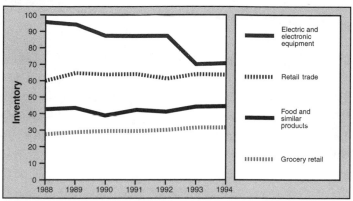

SOURCE: Schonfeld & Associates, *IRS Corporate Financial Ratios.*
Data reflect all reporting profitable businesses with assets over $100 million.

Consider the food manufacturer with 45 days of inventory. Although trade promotions and rapidly changing product lines required maximum flexibility, its manufacturing system was inflexibly geared toward long runs. This mismatch alone resulted in 16 days of inventory.

At the same time, a poor forecasting system added another 15 inventory days, compounding the promotional volatility with requirements for excess safety stock during the peak weeks. High safety-stock requirements, in turn, required manufacturing to produce even further ahead of consumer demand. Ironically, the longer manufacturing lead times made forecasting more difficult.

Finally, to accommodate the high levels of inventory, the company had built a costly physical infrastructure—extra distribution centers, shipping centers, and temporary storage. These facilities added another 14 days.

The bottom line: excess inventory was costing the company millions of dollars a year. By the time the consumer was able to buy the product, about seven weeks after manufacture, much of it had become stale or damaged from multiple handlings.

The diagnostic helped all the company's employees understand that change was necessary, and it gave them a common framework for developing a breakthrough strategy.

Step 2. Start with a clean sheet to redesign processes.

The next step is to integrate supply and demand in your supply chain by carefully balancing six interrelated factors.

1. **Demand volatility.** Manage promotions to reduce volume spikes through such techniques as regionalization and better staggering of promotion cycles. This lowers the capacity required to meet consumer demand while cutting the inventory associated with filling the pipeline.

2. **Forecasting accuracy.** Better forecasting reduces safety stock and stranded inventory in both the retail channel and the manufacturer supply chain. It also allows suppliers to shorten their lead times and reduce their inventories.

3. **Manufacturing flexibility.** Synchronizing manufacturing with consumer demand requires speed, fast changeovers, and machine and labor flexibility in order to make more frequent shorter runs as economical as longer runs had been.

4. **Supplier performance.** Cutting lead times and improving delivery times reduce the safety stock necessary to run the system at high service levels and lower the total cost of supply-chain inputs.

5. **Product design and complexity.** For manufacturers of more complex assembled goods, such as appliances or computers, designing products for both manufacturing and logistics not only lowers direct production costs but also slashes component inventories, shortens supplier response times, and improves service levels. Pruning unnecessary variety and complexity in the SKU portfolio works toward the same ends.

6. **Network design.** Pulling inventory from the system necessitates rethinking the physical distribution network. Often, changes in the preceding variables allow a substantial reduction in facilities and fixed cost.

Breakthrough comes from synchronizing these six variables through statistical process control in a new supply-chain model. The key is linking production, product flow, and inventory levels to the replenishment cycle (supply factors) and to the variability of customer purchases (demand factors). An analogue to statistical process control in plants, this capability embeds analytical rigor and learning in the day-to-day decision-making across the entire supply chain—how much to produce when, and how much inventory to hold for each SKU at each location at any time. (See Exhibit 2.)

The integrated model allows one to evaluate the sensitivity of overall per-

Exhibit 2

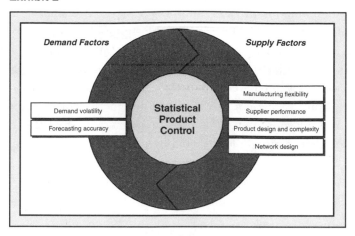

formance to each variable and the effects of interaction across variables—in effect, to establish the laws of physics for the chain. Shortening manufacturing lead times, for example, helps improve the forecasting system, which lowers total system inventory, which helps manufacturing react faster to consumer demand. Understanding these second-order effects leads to a more dramatic redesign.

Step 3. Prototype, modify, and roll out.

Transferring the vision from paper to reality is the downfall of most supply-chain efforts. While it's true that change in one part will affect another, it's not necessary—or advisable—to change everything at once.

Instead, focus on improving the two or three variables with the highest leverage. Initial success will overcome organizational skepticism and build momentum. You can then move on to overhaul the other processes, integrate them, and realize the full potential of the redesigned supply chain.

The food manufacturer, for example, found that its most critical levers were manufacturing flexibility, forecasting accuracy, distribution network design, and statistical product control. The company set up a pilot program to reduce changeover times radically and improve line flexibility in the plants. Within four weeks—and with relatively little capital investment—critical changeovers went from four hours to less than 15 minutes, which allowed the plants to produce smaller, more frequent runs geared to the following week's demand. Meanwhile, the new forecasting process cut the 70 percent forecasting error rate in half. By improving these four areas, the company cut in half its supply-chain inventory.

With its credibility established, the team created a new distribution network design, eliminating five large shipping centers, 35 smaller distribution centers, and an additional 20 percent of the supply-chain inventory.

"Make in a week what you sell in a week" calls for bold, radical improvements in the key parameters of supply-chain performance—99 percent in-stock service levels with half the inventory, logistics costs, and time to market. If, like many, you have experienced more modest incremental improvement, it's time to rethink your approach. A new benchmark is being set—don't let it be the one that sends you to the sidelines.

This article was first published in November 1996.

PRICE BY DESIGN, NOT BY DEFAULT

Michael Grindfors, Matthew A. Krentz, and Henry M. Vogel

Strategic pricing is one of the most powerful sources of profits and growth. Yet, in recent years, it has been the least exploited driver of shareholder value. Few manufacturers review their pricing systematically. Most set prices reactively. Some extrapolate from history, and for others it's just a hunch.

Today the need for strategic pricing is greater than ever. Pressures from price-sensitive consumers on one side, and a forceful and consolidating retail trade on the other, have resulted in significant price rollbacks on everything from cigarettes to cereal. Some claim that the rollbacks have been good for business, but the net result has been considerable profit erosion.

Worse yet, packaged goods manufacturers have lost control of pricing and, with it, the power to position products for profit and growth. Most manufacturers feel locked into current prices for the foreseeable future. "We can't raise prices now—the retailer won't let us," one of them laments. "Price increases mean share loss. If I do it, I'm dead." Another complains, "We don't price strategically anymore. Pricing now is little more than a plug to make our plan numbers."

Strategic pricing recaptures control. A Boston Consulting Group study of more than 1,400 companies with varying profit margins and cost structures concluded that for most companies, an increase in net price of only 1 or 2 percent is enough to boost profits by 25 to 50 percent (see Exhibit 3).

Exhibit 3

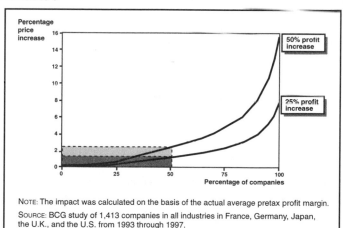

NOTE: The impact was calculated on the basis of the actual average pretax profit margin.

SOURCE: BCG study of 1,413 companies in all industries in France, Germany, Japan, the U.K., and the U.S. from 1993 through 1997.

Executed correctly, strategic pricing can

- boost total profitability by pricing on the basis of consumers' long-term demand elasticity

- increase sales of a company's most profitable products

- improve the profitability of noncore businesses

- stop price leaks by monitoring price concessions

- create competitive advantage that is hard to imitate

Regaining control of prices, however, won't be easy. In most organizations, pricing power is diffused among many players making countless decisions across multiple functions and locations. Today no manager knows precisely what portion of any list price is actually realized. That means he or she can't position the product for the greatest return when making pricing decisions.

There's no way around the fact that pricing is complex—too complex for quick fixes. Instead, manufacturers need to designate a SWAT team of senior managers to rethink all aspects of pricing—strategies, tactics, processes, and capabilities—from the ground up. To succeed, the team must integrate four activities.

Discover the Product's Value Equation

Every product has an implied *value equation*, which takes into account the relationship between its quality, convenience, and price. This relationship will vary for different consumer segments. To price strategically, the SWAT team must understand the role that price plays in the product's value and competitive landscape.

The team's first job is to analyze their products' value equations and benchmark them against the competition's. The team should investigate

- product positioning, which includes brand value, relative share position, and private-label development

- competitive landscape, which includes the pricing supply curve, relative cost structure, and market discipline (leaders and followers)

- consumer motivation, which includes segmentation of needs and benefits, long-term price elasticity, the impulse-buying dynamic, and life-cycle profitability in each segment

The objective is to ensure that the pricing structure both supports the value equation and captures the full value of any advantages in cost, quality, or service. We call this "pricing to your sweet spot." If, for instance, the product is the only one of its kind to feature a warranty that consumers particularly value, it should be priced accordingly. Such a strategy goes beyond traditional pricing tactics to recognize the value of a product that can be realized in the marketplace.

Take the example of a beverage producer, which we'll call Company A. It learned a painful lesson in sweet-spot pricing from its chief competitor, the national leader. As the leader began to lower prices in A's highest-share markets, A's regional managers assumed they had no choice but to follow suit. What the managers didn't realize, however, was that the leader was simultaneously *raising* prices in its own highest-share markets. In fact, the leader's strategy was to increase prices and margins in its strongest markets in order to subsidize its campaign to gain share where it was disadvantaged. Company A fell right into the trap: the leader not only increased its profits and overall share, but it also drained profits from A's strongest markets.

Plug the Price Leaks

Generic pricing often conceals differences in the cost of serving customers and can distort the net profitability delivered by channel, customer, and product. The SWAT team must discover the price leaks where profits are being lost. This involves tracking all the contractual and noncontractual discounts, promotions, and other costs of serving customers (such as finance charges, warehousing and delivery costs, and administrative costs) that siphon off revenues.

Price leaks can be found throughout the company. Often, they are hidden in unexpected places or misperceived as the cost of doing business with customers. These "costs" should be examined with the same de-averaging tools that accountants and manufacturers use to examine product profitability. Once the team determines the true profitability of each account, opportunities for strategic pricing will surface. Companies that have systematically plugged their leaks have seen their profits increase by as much as 25 percent.

One BCG client, for example, was asked by its largest customer to bypass the distribution center and deliver directly to stores. Fulfilling this request would have involved picking individual cases instead of pallets and sending out less than full truckloads (LTL). Other vendors had granted the request in order to preserve the account relationship. Our client's account manager, however, was aware of the costs involved in this concession and was able to negotiate a better price. As a result, our client has begun to introduce "menu pricing" to its customers, in which higher-cost services, such as case picks and LTL shipments, are an option in the pricing structure.

Negotiate Prices for Profits

Integrating the pieces of the pricing puzzle will also reveal opportunities to improve the productivity of promotions. In recent years, promotions have increased, and spending on off-invoice discounting, price exceptions, promotional allowances, merchandising funds, and rebates has grown dramatically. One BCG client discovered that the total cost of its deals was more than 20 percent of sales. Too often, promotions amount to price leaks rather than investments. Although some promotions pay off, many merely transfer value to retailers and to consumers who forward-buy.

Negotiating deals by using simplistic rules of thumb, such as number of cases shipped to retailers, can be misleading and expensive. Instead, negotiations and, for some retailers, payments should be based on true incremental volume actually sold to consumers. To do this, the SWAT team must review trade spending to determine the total return on investment. It also needs to determine its promotion strategy in the context of the retailer's pricing strategies. Differences in retailer pricing strategies (everyday low prices versus high-low pricing, for instance) and the margins that retailers take on various products will significantly affect a manufacturer's negotiating power and posture.

Organize to Streamline the Process

No pricing strategy will work for long without a well-managed process. The SWAT team should reach down in the organization, define clear roles and responsibilities, and make sure the right information is always available to the people who need it.

Why do senior managers need to get so deeply involved? Several parts of the organization play a role in pricing, but it takes executive clout to synchronize all the levers, nail down the tactical side, and make the tough strategic decisions. A few companies have already moved in this direction by appointing a pricing czar and council to integrate pricing data and streamline decisions. This doesn't centralize authority over pricing as much as manage the dissemination of information that others need in order to make the right decisions.

BCG recently helped an office products manufacturer to surface its pricing data so that a pricing council could improve price realization and make consistent strategic and tactical decisions. Meeting quarterly, the council monitors movement in the price of raw materials and analyzes portfolio mix, account-pricing strategy, and profitability. On the basis of this information, the company redesigned its pricing structure and renegotiated its trade deals and rebate programs to focus on performance. It also established a new process for authorizing price exceptions. In addition to helping the company win back control over its prices, the streamlined process saved costs by eliminating rework and reducing administrative expenses. As a result, the company increased its bottom line by several percentage points.

Getting Started

Although most companies have focused on cost reduction, strategic pricing is a much more powerful way to increase profits. Is your company missing the opportunity to boost profits by as much as 50 percent? These four questions can serve as a quick audit of your pricing capabilities:

1. Do our competitors' pricing strategies seem irrational or inconsistent, or could they be part of a winning strategy?

2. Do we suspect price leaks, and if so, do we know where and how big they are?

3. Do we control all aspects of our pricing process?

4. Do we price by default or by design?

Strategic pricing isn't a one-time tactic; it's a fundamental restructuring of all activities that affect pricing. That's why it offers long-term, sustainable value. And there's another, more subtle benefit. Because the restructuring occurs deep within the organization, it is nearly impossible for competitors to imitate.

This article was first published in June 1998.

Rebekah Padgett and Philip Siegel

The track record for customer-supplier partnerships hasn't been good. It's not that the participants lack commitment but that they have no process to help them form mutually rewarding partnerships. An approach that we call "discovery" is such a process. By using fact-based analysis and information technology, it has transformed purchasing-department contacts into broader, deeper relationships and helped suppliers and customers create new value in their businesses.

Partnerships that use discovery are especially powerful in the consumer goods and retail industry because of its low degree of vertical integration. Retailers rely on manufacturers, wholesalers, and distributors for their products. Manufacturers need retailers for access to end users. Such value-chain interdependence increases the opportunities for discovery partnerships, which in turn can lead to new sources of profits.

What Makes Discovery Different?

Traditional customer-supplier partnerships focus on supply-chain handoffs and on the interactions between customers and sales reps or administrative staff. The discovery process goes behind those obvious contact points to explore the issues that affect the handoffs, such as consumer usage, retail merchandising, promotional effectiveness, and pricing. It accomplishes this with an investigative team comprising people from a range of functions in both the supplier and customer organizations.

When players from all parts of the value chain work together, it's easy to identify overlapping services. But that's only the beginning. Discovery goes beyond such cost-reduction tactics to find opportunities for increasing revenues and improving entire processes.

Moreover, discovery is grounded in facts. In most cases, by the time people are called together to solve a problem, the problem is approaching a crisis. In such an atmosphere, it doesn't take long for accusations and excuses to start flying. Generalizations are made without data to support them. Decisions are reactive and emotional.

Because the discovery process requires rigorous analysis and fact gathering, it reduces tension and promotes cooperation. If a customer's marketing head claims that the problem is in the packaging, he'd better be able to prove it. If the supplier's sales rep says the manufacturer isn't managing the product specs, she needs to supply evidence.

Putting Discovery into Practice

Consider the relationship between a U.S. truck manufacturer with nationwide dealerships and one of its suppliers, an independent finance company that provides credit to dealers and consumers. The manufacturer was unhappy with its market share, and the finance company was unhappy with its penetration of loans. Each suspected that the other was responsible for its problems.

For the discovery effort, the two companies formed a team composed of people from their marketing, sales, and product development departments. As they went through the data, the real causes and solutions emerged. The team learned that the loan approval process was very slow. The main reason was that the forms used by the truck dealers were inconsistent with those used by the loan company's branches. The solution was to standardize the forms.

Having solved that problem, the team went further, looking at customer retention. In analyzing what kinds of information each company gathered about its customers, the team learned that the finance company knew when truck loans were to be paid off and the truck company knew the repair records of its customers' trucks. The team put this information together to come up with a powerful strategy: target customers would receive personal notes about new vehicles in stock and about special financing they could obtain. The strategy has been a win for both companies.

But the team didn't stop there. It discovered that both companies could reap considerable value from combining certain back-office operations. To that end, the manufacturer turned over to the finance company many of the functions it had performed on its own.

Finally, the discovery process itself highlighted the need for more communication between the organizations. Neither company knew, for instance, when the other was bringing out a new product. As the team began to discuss the problem, the truck manufacturer's product manager revealed that the company was planning to launch a new model that month, and the loan company's manager responded that his company had data on the new model's market segment. As a result of those findings, the companies are planning a joint launch, including a financial product designed specifically for buyers of the new truck. Both expect a considerable increase in revenues.

How Can Discovery Help You?

As the example illustrates, discovery stretches both organizations. Senior managers become more active in customer relationships, and team members search for innovative solutions. Discovery reduces conflict, improves understanding, and creates powerful new alliances for both suppliers and customers.

The process isn't for the faint-hearted, however. The scope of the investigation and the depth of analysis require trust and hard work. Nevertheless, The Boston Consulting Group has conducted more than 100 discoveries around the world, and in almost every case, suppliers and customers have been excited to find how much value they can create together.

Discovery begins when your company is able to answer tough questions such as the ones below. Detailed, specific, fact-based responses will challenge you to stop and think about opportunities that have gone undiscovered in your value chain.

1. Can you describe in detail your customers' and suppliers' product portfolios, cost structures, and sources of profitability, growth, and competitive differentiation?   YES ☐   NO ☐   MAYBE ☐

2. Do you understand how your product influences different aspects of the value chain, such as production processes, logistics, and quality?   YES ☐   NO ☐   MAYBE ☐

3. Can you describe how your customers' and suppliers' demand will shift over the next five years? What products will be introduced and when? What the new sources of value will be?   YES ☐   NO ☐   MAYBE ☐

4. Do you know your current share of volume and dollars across all possible service offerings?   YES ☐   NO ☐   MAYBE ☐

5. Do you understand the time and costs in your customers' and suppliers' product-delivery systems from   YES ☐   NO ☐   MAYBE ☐

raw material through processing, inventory, distribution, consumption, and the reorder cycle? Do you know where the redundancies and time or cost losses are?

6. Can you describe how your end users could be served cheaper or better? Can you describe a stream of product improvements that you could implement for your customers or that your suppliers could implement for you?

    YES   NO   MAYBE

    ☐   ☐   ☐

7. Do you know when and why you win bids, and how your customers make their decisions?

    YES   NO   MAYBE

    ☐   ☐   ☐

8. Do you know how much your customers and suppliers would value each potential product improvement?

    YES   NO   MAYBE

    ☐   ☐   ☐

9. Can you analyze your customers' organizations—their relationships with their customers, the frequency of contacts, and how they position their products? Can your suppliers do this for your organization?

    YES   NO   MAYBE

    ☐   ☐   ☐

10. Do you know what strategic alliance or product development breakthrough would increase your share and how it would affect your customers and suppliers?

    YES   NO   MAYBE

    ☐   ☐   ☐

This article was first published in October 1998.

David C. Edelman and Dieter Heuskel

Powerful forces, driven by the information revolution, are undermining many vertically integrated consumer-goods companies. Contract manu-facturers and logistics specialists, as well as power-branding strategies and increasingly demanding capital markets, are rapidly deconstructing and reconstructing the traditional value chain.

Information has always been the glue that has held value chains together. The cost of getting sufficiently rich information to suppliers, distribution channels, and customers has given vertical integration its leverage. As transaction costs plummet, that glue is dissolving. Increasingly, universal access to rich information and common communications standards are enabling the open and virtually free exchange of all kinds of information. Companies are sharing product designs, CAD/CAM parameters, logistics information, and financial data with equal ease inside and outside the corporation. Manufacturers and their suppliers are communicating *and* collaborating more than ever before. The walls that divided companies are collapsing.

This shift is giving birth to at least two strategic options for consumer goods companies: becoming a power brander, which orchestrates a network of suppliers for nonstrategic or particularly capital-intensive parts of the value chain, or becoming a "layer player," which uses dominance of a single layer of the value chain to enter other industries.

Before deconstruction, a company could maintain an advantage if the average productivity of all the activities it performed was higher than that of its competitors. Today a company must excel in every activity because every link of its value chain is being challenged. That doesn't mean that integrated manufacturers will disappear altogether, but they must be highly productive in everything they do. Otherwise, they should be ready to deconstruct.

A notable example of deconstruction is Sara Lee's recent move to spin off the manufacturing division of the apparel company. The strategy permitted the apparel company to enjoy the benefits of an international supply network and forced the spun-off manufacturing company to improve its performance by exposing it to market competition. Consumer goods companies need to be aware of such business models and assess their own options for unlocking shareholder value by paring back to the activities that yield the highest returns.

The Orchestrators

Power branders have been around for decades in the fashion and food industries. But because deconstruction lets virtually any kind of company attain high levels of productivity with few assets, power branders are now cropping up in hard goods, magazines and TV, furniture, sporting goods, and domestics. Highly successful power branders, such as Nike, Adidas, Martha Stewart, and ConAgra's Healthy Choice, *orchestrate* suppliers and partners to deliver consistently high quality in a variety of products under a single robust brand.

Power branders that excel in orchestration enjoy two advantages. First, outsourcing nonessential activities allows them to be flexible and responsive to shifting tastes; and second, the proliferation of the brand name across many kinds of products gives them economies of scale in marketing the brand. Martha Stewart's ability to orchestrate a complex network of suppliers, coupled with its enormous marketing power in television and the print media, have made the company the second largest marketer of bed and bath textiles, and a trendsetter in home fashions, with sales of $800 million in 1998.

The Layer Players

Lacking the brand recognition of a power brander, some companies with single-category brands are turning to horizontal strategies. Westpoint Stevens, one of the largest manufacturers of bed and bath textiles, still produces its own brand, Martex, for the high-end market in department sotres. Increasingly, however, the company is providing services for others. Toward that end, Westpoint recently enhanced its supply capabilities by purchasing Liebhardt Mills, a leading manufacturer of private-label bedding products. And Westpoint has added Joe Boxer and Esprit to its list of private-label clients, which includes Wal-Mart and Target.

In Europe, Lufthansa and Swissair have both focused on building strong positions in the catering layer of the airline business, where they are the top two competitors. They've managed to grow their businesses *and* shareholder value substantially by taking their expertise outside their own companies.

Deconstruction raises several issues for consumer goods manufacturers: What to own? What to buy? What to sell? Whom to buy from? Whom to partner with? To make the right decisions, companies must thoroughly analyze their businesses as well as their ability to execute a new strategy. As Exhibit 4 indicates, companies must weigh the pros and cons of deconstruction at every link of the value chain.

Exhibit 4

To Deconstruct or Not to Deconstruct

	Design >	Production >	Distribution >	Marketing >	Sales
Opportunities	When freelance talent is available	When scale advantage is minimal	When shared networks emerge	Whan a power brand has a franchise	When shared brokers emerge
	When specialists in components emerge	When there is overcapacity in the company	When on-line channels emerge	When private-label suppliers emerge	When e-commerce emerges
Risks	Designers could go directly to market	Products could be commoditized	Business could get locked into a distributor's process and standards	The franchise could lose power	Brand value could become diluted with the use of an outside sales force
	Designers could develop their own brand	Cost advantage could disappear	Power could shift to retailers	The brand could become overexposed	Consumer comparison shopping could trigger a price or feature war

Examining the Options

Here are some moves a company might consider as it appraises its performance in the new environment:

Outsource or leverage manufacturing. If the industry is shifting from large-scale, low-cost manufacturing to flexible, fast-response products, assembling a network of suppliers with excellent production capabilities may be the best move. As scale benefits erode, it becomes easier and cheaper to reverse engineer, copy, and produce short runs of new products. A supplier's flexibility and responsiveness, therefore, matter more today in many categories than scale does. Before taking such a drastic step as outsourcing the manufacturing function, a company should understand its effect on technology flows and cost position, and realize that competitors will have access to the same suppliers. If the company itself has superior production capabilities but not brand potential, opportunities abound for it to become a supplier through private-label agreements.

Outsource or leverage innovation or technology. If the industry's most successful products are coming from external design and technology firms, it may make sense to tap that talent. Companies that outsource, however, should make sure they have a marketing and distribution advantage to prevent designers from getting between the company and its customers. Design companies such as IDEO and Frog Design, which have no manufacturing or marketing capability, can supply high-quality services to companies that excel in those downstream functions. A company with superior design capabilities could decide to leverage its own technology by selling or licensing it on the open market. Procter & Gamble, for example, discovered a process for adding calcium to citrus juices, but the company licenses it to other makers of fruit juices instead of using it exclusively for its own brand.

Outsource or leverage distribution. If a company's in-house delivery capabilities are falling behind its competitors', it should consider going outside the company. But companies that decide to outsource should recognize that using a supplier's standards decreases their ability to achieve advantage through customized service. Logistics specialists, such as Federal Express and UPS, are focusing on speed and flexibility to serve a broad range of industries. These alternative distribution channels offer turnkey warehouse and fulfillment services including pick and pack, as well as traditional package delivery. Outsourcing distribution can be a relatively easy move, and scale players often provide better and lower-cost services. Of course, if a company's delivery capabilities are much better than its competitors', it could decide to become a layer player.

Leverage brand power. If a brand is strong enough to cover a variety of products, the company may decide to become a power brander. With scale advantage shifting from manufacturing to marketing, power branders can amortize their marketing investment across a broad range of products while outsourcing production and logistics. In the U.K., supermarket brands are becoming serous competitors in financial services, and the Virgin label continues to attack new sectors with aplomb. But power branders must recognize the totality of risk if the brand loses power. Consider Nike, whose expansion from shoes to other athletic products generated phenomenal corporate growth. Recently, however, Nike has been threatened by competitors attacking its core sneaker franchise.

Analyze, Reflect, Act

As new markets appear at every link in the value chain, the logic of a vertically integrated company must be continually proved rather than taken for granted. Deconstruction *is* having a considerable impact. But taking apart a value chain is a radical decision. It could mean transforming a company into a collection of independent businesses that buy and sell on the open market.

The key is knowing what you do best. If you are the low-cost manufacturer, could you gain leverage by producing for all players? If your brand can extend into new areas, could you create a licensing and management infrastructure? If you have technology that is applicable across disparate businesses, could you create a strategy to capture that value?

Many integrated manufacturers will continue in their traditional forms. But they should be aware of the threats and opportunities that increasing numbers of networked businesses will present. The goal isn't necessarily to break a company apart; it is to make each layer of the value chain as productive as it can be. Taking a deconstructive view is the first step.

This article was first published in May 1999.

STARTING FRESH: TAKING A VALUE APPROACH TO COSTS

Katrina Helmkamp and Jacques Chapuis

 A lot of companies agonize over it—only a few do it. To be sure, taking a fresh, holistic approach to overhead costs is a daunting task. But consider this: the consumer doesn't want to pay for administration. The consumer doesn't want to pay for financial audits. The consumer doesn't want to pay for billing processes. Companies that take a surgical approach to their cost structures discover three things:

1. A considerable percentage of total overhead does not generate value.

2. A considerable percentage of total overhead could be revamped to increase value.

3. The list of what the company isn't doing but should be doing is extensive. It includes activities that could increase strategic advantage if only *someone* would take the initiative.

We have developed a process for performing a comprehensive review of overhead costs, which we call value-based cost reduction (VCR). Unlike conventional reengineering efforts and across-the-board cost cuts, VCR directs companies to take a fresh look at all their support activities to determine which ones add value for *customers* and which simply need to get done. The goal is to identify the low-value activities that can be eliminated or performed more efficiently and the high-value activities that help fulfill the company's goals and may require increased resources.

VCR is much more than basic cost reduction because it identifies not only what can be cut but also what needs to be added to create a stronger company. Moreover, VCR can revitalize mature businesses by helping them recapture the intensity and focus of their start-up days.

Minimalist or Activist Headquarters?

At the headquarters of many global consumer-goods companies, you're likely to find an uninspired staff performing numerous checks and balances on the business units. Despite regular housecleaning, more and more people seem to be hired to produce less and less real value. A typical reengineering approach would strive for standardized processes and minimal staffing for each and every support function. VCR, on the other hand, seeks to identify, enhance, and nurture the activities that deliver strategic value to the business units. VCR's goal, therefore, is to apply a *minimalist* approach to noncore, or low-value, support activities and an *activist* approach to critical components of the corporate center (see Exhibit 5).

Generally, low-value support activities include such back-office functions as accounting, finance, information services, and some areas of human resources. The work that occurs in those functions—paying bills, performing tax audits, maintaining employee records, ordering office supplies—is necessary to the business but doesn't directly affect the consumer's experience of the company's offering. No one buys a product because of those activities. Therefore, any cost above what is required to get the job done is a drain on the company's margins and its capacity for investment.

The challenge, of course, is to separate necessary from unnecessary costs. This is where the clean slate comes in: the fundamental rule of VCR is, Don't presume anything and question everything. To avoid the turf battles that inevitably arise when efficiencies are questioned, VCR considers each activity from several different viewpoints. The process includes

- a baseline analysis of how much time is spent on major activities

- interviews with functional support managers to pinpoint the activities they think can be streamlined

Exhibit 5

VCR Versus Reengineering

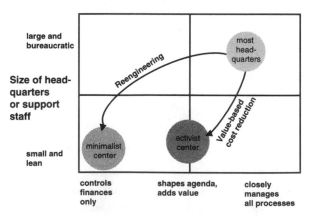

Focus of headquarters or support staff

- interviews with the people who perform the activities to identify causes of rework

- interviews with the internal customers of the activities to determine value added

- benchmarks from other areas of the company

- benchmarks from other companies

When people feel that they have hit a wall and can't streamline activities any further, internal benchmarks often prove as compelling as, or even more compelling than, external ones. Evidence that another business unit within the company can perform the same activity at a lower cost is an excellent tool for prodding people to rethink their assumptions.

Creating an Activist Headquarters

An activist headquarters may be nearly as lean as a minimalist headquarters—often with only 50 to 100 people. Unlike a minimalist center, though, it will explicitly identify, enhance, and nurture activities that add demonstrable value to the business units. These activities will vary according to a company's strategy. Consider the following examples:

- A company planning to grow through acquisitions would benefit from an activist merger-and-acquisition function.

- A company distributing goods in 30 countries might designate its global logistics and supply-chain function as activist.

- Nearly all consumer goods and services companies would identify product-innovation and global-rollout capabilities as activist. A headquarters that fosters innovation and facilitates the rapid introduction of new products around the world drives growth in the marketplace.

Once particular functions are designated as activist, there is, of course, the danger that they will become mini-empires. To prevent that from happening, VCR requires the manger of an activist function to build a business case and demonstrate a return on investment before receiving additional funds.

Promising Results

Having seen the disappointing results of across-the-board cuts and reengineering efforts, many companies have started experimenting with value-based cost reduction. So far, the results have been impressive: at companies that have taken a VCR approach, staff has been reduced by 15 to 30 percent and expenses have been cut by 15 to 25 percent. And the streamlined headquarters have been able to support the corporate strategy and drive growth.

VCR should not be a one-time event. Once the process is under way, it should become a way of doing business year in and year out. Here are the kinds of questions that managers at VCR companies ask themselves on a daily basis:

- Can the business units pinpoint areas where headquarters adds value?

- Which support functions are not of high value to internal customers?

- Which support functions should we minimize? Which do we need to streamline or eliminate? Do key customers agree to the changes?

- Have we identified activist functions that support our strategy? Have we allocated sufficient resources to those activities? Are we seeing high returns on our investments in them?

The corporate centers of consumer goods companies must renew their responsibility to reduce costs, increase value, and make the whole enterprise greater than the sum of its parts. Regular top-to-bottom reviews are no longer an option—they're a requirement for success. Funds freed from performing checks and balances can be redeployed to nurture innovation, gain insight into consumers, and develop new products and services.

This article was first published in September 1999.

Marin Gjaja and Henry M. Vogel

Direct store delivery (DSD) is one of the most misunderstood and undervalued segments of the retail supply chain. Many retailers believe that DSD means giving up control of their stores to an army of outsiders and putting their destiny in someone else's hands. Others think that DSD vendors clog the back doors and create more paperwork than profits. They view DSD as a high-cost, inefficient distribution system that will disappear over time.

Such conventional thinking is wrong. It does not appreciate the fundamental power and economics of DSD. In fact, for many food manufacturers and most retailers, DSD is the best bet for securing growth and profit in a highly competitive environment.

In a study of the grocery supply chain conducted for the Grocery Manufacturers Association, The Boston Consulting Group found solid evidence that DSD can result in increased sales and higher profits. Trained, focused, and motivated DSD sales reps, supported by manufacturers' expertise in national category trends and consumer needs, can generate

- faster sales turns and velocity

- higher incremental lift from promotions

- fewer "out-of-stocks" and fresher products due to more frequent replenishment

- better service through in-store category management

- greater value for consumers

To be sure, DSD isn't the answer for every retail category or product, and it still has some problems to overcome. Nevertheless, it can deliver profit and growth disproportionate to the amount of shelf space its products occupy. One recent study of the top 100 food categories in a major supermarket chain found that while DSD items represented only 20 percent of store space, they delivered nearly 25 percent of sales and generated more than 50 percent of profits. Given the current state of the grocery industry—relatively flat sales, increasing capacity, diminishing productivity, new competition from emerging channels such as the Internet, and the race to find and pay for partnerships to compete with Wal-Mart—leveraging DSD as a strategic weapon will be essential for both retailers and manufacturers.

DSD Delivers Sales, Service, and Satisfaction

Between 1993 and 1998, sales of DSD categories grew more than 3 percent per year, while most warehouse-delivered categories barely inched above 1 percent. Moreover, of the top 20 consumer packaged-goods companies, the DSD suppliers delivered even greater growth. Although sales of these companies' products represent only about one-third of the total, they grew more than four times faster than sales of products that were distributed through the grocery warehouse system. (See Exhibit 6.) As a group, DSD companies delivered more than $5 billion in sales, or two-thirds of the total growth.

The explanation for this remarkable growth lies in both the product characteristics and consumer dynamics of DSD categories, as well as in the ability of DSD suppliers to exploit them. Because of their short shelf life, low value density, high velocity, and demand variability, DSD products require focused attention. DSD categories, such as salty snacks, tend to be "consumption elastic"—purchased on impulse and consumed rapidly. As most retailers know, these impulse purchases can contribute to significant sales and profit growth. However, it takes attentive service to keep the shelves stocked and attractive. As one retailer puts it, "A lost impulse sale is lost forever."

DSD systems are nimble and can handle the sales peaks and valleys resulting from intense promotion activity. And DSD reps provide the focus and high

Exhibit 6

DSD Suppliers Deliver Faster Growth

Top 20 U.S. consumer packaged-goods suppliers[1]

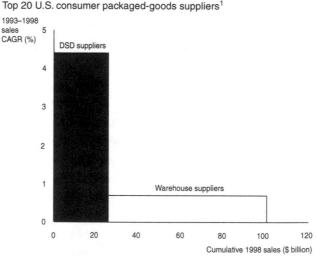

Source: IRI;BCG analysis

[1] IRI ranking according to 1998 U.S. sales; supermarket channel only.

service levels that can minimize out-of-stocks. Unlike a stock boy who earns an hourly wage, DSD reps are motivated to do the extra work. To quote another retailer, "They romance the displays to maximize impulse sales." As a result, leading DSD brands generate as much as three times the incremental lift from promotions as warehouse-delivered private-label or branded products.

One retailer and one DSD supplier we worked with discovered DSD's power to increase sales when they experimented with DSD distribution in a few stores but continued with warehouse distribution in the others. They found that sales growth was seven points higher in the DSD stores. In addition, the DSD merchandisers actually grew the overall category and not just their own sales, while the category stagnated in the non-DSD stores.

DSD Delivers Higher Profits

Sales growth is a powerful element in the DSD dynamic, but it is not the whole story. One reason DSD is so misunderstood is that retailers tend to focus on gross profit. Although easy to calculate, this measure can be very misleading when one tries to understand a product's true economic performance. The retail supply chain is loaded with direct and incremental costs for getting products from the receiving dock to the retail shelf, and these don't appear in gross profit margins. As a result, as sales volumes increase, so do the retailer's operating expenses. DSD doesn't just reduce those costs; it eliminates them.

We believe that calculating the contribution margin, rather than gross profit, is a better way to measure a retailer's true profit. The contribution margin is what remains after direct and incremental costs are deducted from gross profit. In other words, it is what's left over that can *contribute* to covering fixed store and overhead expenses.

By using activity-based costing (ABC), we were able to quantify the direct and incremental costs that both retailers and manufacturers incur along the entire supply chain. These costs include

- labor at the distribution center to receive, warehouse, pick, check, and ship the product

- in-store labor to order, stock, rotate, and merchandise; to build displays; and to manage inventory, space, and promotions

- additional warehouse space, fleet capacity, and specialized equipment—rented or built—to handle such bulky DSD items as beer, soft drinks, and salty snacks

- complexity costs in the store and warehouse resulting from demand variability

Overall, DSD vendors contribute more than 150 million labor hours per year to the grocery trade. That amounts to over 100 hours of "free" labor per week for the average store. If store managers had to recruit, manage, and pay for this legion of workers, the cost would likely reduce their after-tax operating profit by more than 45 percent.

Measuring contribution profitability can reveal some startling facts. In one recent study, several of the categories with the highest gross margins were actually *losing* money at the contribution profit level. Many of the products in those categories were warehouse delivered, which means the retailer incurred the incremental costs to warehouse, deliver, and stock the shelves. With DSD-delivered products, the retailer's only costs are the administrative expense of receiving the product in the store's back room and the terms it negotiates with its suppliers.

When the study compared the contribution margins of DSD and warehouse-delivered categories, DSD categories ranked at the top. The average contribution margin was more than ten percentage points higher for DSD categories (14.3 percent) than for warehouse-delivered categories. And in categories with mixed distribution, DSD products consistently outperformed products going through the retailer's warehouse.

For example, when the leading DSD salty-snack brand was compared with the leading warehouse-delivered salty-snack brand, the DSD brand generated both a higher gross margin *and* a higher contribution margin. In fact, the contribution margin was more than 40 percent higher for the leading DSD brand. (See Exhibit 7.)

DSD Delivers Productivity and Shareholder Value

Retailers who understand the DSD dynamic leverage its power. They allocate space to DSD categories and work with DSD vendors to improve productivity. They understand the true profitability of their categories and products. Retailers who don't understand DSD can end up spending too much time and space on money-losing categories or on underperforming warehouse-delivered substitutes in DSD categories. Although the warehouse products may have higher gross margins, they are less likely to have higher contribution margins and are almost certainly less likely to capture the full potential from impulse sales.

In addition to delivering high contribution margins, DSD products perform well on other critical financial measures. When it comes to sales turns,

Exhibit 7

DSD Categories Deliver Higher Contribution Margins

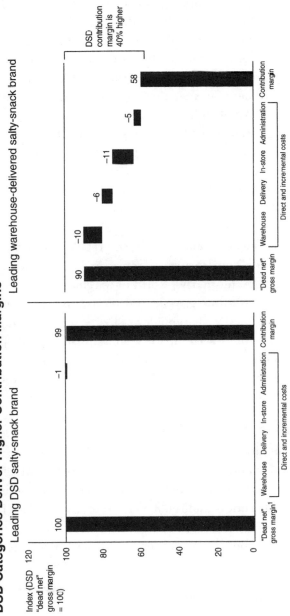

SOURCE: Grocery Manufacturers Association/DSD committee members; BCG estimates and analysis.

1 Gross margin net of markdowns and manufacturer support.

cash flow, and return on working capital, assets, and space, DSD products are clear winners. In the six leading DSD categories, DSD products have an average velocity one and a half times greater than that of warehouse-delivered products. And in the top three categories—beer, cookies, and salty snacks—DSD products sell, on average, three to four times faster.

That velocity generates significant cash flow, which translates into higher returns on inventory and capital. In fact, many retailers actually have *negative* working capital in DSD products. With DSD there is no warehouse inventory to finance, and retailers often hold very few days of inventory in-store. Moreover, the retailer entirely avoids the fixed capital investment of specialized trucks and equipment, as well as additional warehouse space.

Often, DSD products can be sold off the shelves four or five times before retailers must pay for the initial order. Warehoused products, on the other hand, frequently spend a few weeks in the retailer's pipeline even before they get to the store. Then they spend more time on the shelf, forcing retailers to finance several more days' worth of warehouse-delivered products.

The superior cash flow, growth, and return on capital that DSD delivers translate into superior shareholder value for retailers. Our studies indicate that DSD products account for a substantially higher proportion of retailers' operating performance and market capitalization than would be indicated by their proportion of sales alone. DSD is therefore one of the best levers available to grocery retailers for increasing shareholder value.

Harnessing the Power of DSD

Although the numbers are impressive, DSD still has some obstacles to overcome. On the demand side, DSD vendors need to continue improving in-stock conditions, assortment optimization, and merchandising. On the supply side, DSD vendors and retailers need to work together to minimize activities that don't add value, such as back-room check-in, invoice errors, and paper transactions. Many of these problems are being solved by new technologies and procedures that will align supply with demand at the point of sale and make the relationship between retailers and vendors more efficient.

Here are five questions that grocery retailers should ask themselves to ensure that they are leveraging the full power of DSD:

1. Am I capturing the full potential of consumption-elastic categories?

2. Am I allocating space to enhance my store's productivity?

3. Am I focusing on the right categories and products to drive growth?

4. Am I making informed decisions about which products deliver the highest profits?

5. Am I working with my DSD suppliers to minimize the logistical and administrative hurdles in the back room?

More and more grocers are increasing sales, productivity, and profits with DSD. By working together, retailers and leading DSD suppliers can quickly improve the system's effectiveness and efficiency—making tomorrow's results even better than today's.

This article was first published in October 1999.

Part Two

RETAILING

REINVIGORATING THE CORE: THE RETAILER'S CHALLENGE

Felix Barber

Throughout the U.S. and Europe, once-booming retail chains are encountering rapidly maturing markets. As a result, some major players have suffered losses in share value of as much as 40 percent. Historically, mature retailers have generally been unable or unwilling to innovate rapidly enough to maintain their edge. The big U.S. general merchandise chains are a case in point. In the early 1980s, J.C. Penney transformed its chain into a national department store through innovation. But both Sears U.S. and Woolworth tried to mask poor performance in their core businesses with diversification—only to discover that a struggling base business can bring down even the healthiest of sidelines. Releasing most of those acquisitions in the 1990s, Sears learned an important lesson: there's no substitute for innovation at the core.

Understanding What Newcomers Do Differently

Today, transforming a mature retail formula is harder than ever. Simply finding new formats or products isn't enough. New competitors are redesigning the value chain so that the once-clear distinctions between producer, designer, manufacturer, and retailer have almost disappeared. Take Zara, Europe's fastest-growing fashion retailer. In an industry where consumers' tastes are constantly changing, Zara repeatedly offers ahead-of-the-curve trends without the high costs of unsold inventory that most stores have to absorb. Zara has a three-week factory-to-store cycle (the industry average is 6 to 12 months), which allows it to give customers what they want when they want it.

The key to Zara's responsiveness is built into its organization. The company designed and organized its entire product cycle—from fashion design to manufacture, distribution, and sales—to be tightly integrated. This allows Zara to apply state-of-the-art techniques such as CAD and CAM and to link them throughout the value chain. Through the integrated product cycle, Zara limits the materials required for replenishing fast-moving items and ensures availability at all times—a perpetual struggle for its competitors. What's more, Zara's integration streamlines traditional functions. As a fully integrated company, Zara does not need a separate buying department;

instead, category managers and designers make up the merchandise-building team that hands off directly to production.

Building New Skills and Processes

Of course, Zara had the advantage of building its organization from scratch. For older retailers with entrenched cultures and outmoded processes, organizational upheaval can be daunting. It may take, for instance, considerable investment in skill platforms that does not pay back immediately. Managers may have to become experts in areas of the value chain where they currently have limited experience, such as

- efficient consumer response (changing the producer-retailer interface)

- database marketing and home shopping (changing the retailer-consumer interface)

- private-label and vertical brands (changing the producer-retailer-consumer interfaces)

- multichannel and international retailing (greatly increasing the complexity of the retailer's product selection function)

Taking Time, Sustaining Commitment

Does this mean that it's all but impossible for a mature retailer to stay competitive? No, but it does mean that it takes more commitment to organizational change than most retailers anticipate. Just how much commitment can be seen in the story of Tesco, a U.K. supermarket chain that fought long and hard to regain its place at the top.

Tesco began its successful run in the 1960s with a classic "pile 'em high and sell 'em cheap" discount formula. But in the late 1970s it was challenged by Sainsbury's high-quality store label and ASDA's larger stores, broader ranges, and ample parking. Tesco rapidly went from leader to trailer. It responded by looking not only at what its competitors were doing for the customer but also at how they did it. To compete, Tesco realized, it needed to double its store size and restructure its whole organization to establish a reputation for food quality and a strong private-label program.

Then it went further with new formats to capture small-town and convenience shoppers not reached by its superstores, with an efficient consumer response (ECR) program founded on sales-based reordering and EDI, and with a series of smaller innovations, such as a frequent-buyer program that put zip into its marketing message.

Tesco is now back in the game, but it didn't happen overnight. In fact, it took the better part of ten years, a massive organizational transformation, and a long period of shaken investor confidence.

Surviving the Leadership Challenge

Tesco's comeback illustrates three important lessons. First, responding to customers depends directly on having the right organizational capabilities in place. Second, it takes considerable time and resources—especially for mature retailers—to establish those capabilities. Tesco's strategy created enormous opening and closing costs, putting significant pressure on performance. The food-quality and own-brand programs required new skills and a reorganization of buying and marketing. Similarly, the move to ECR entailed more powerful information technology and logistics capabilities. The third lesson is that major innovation takes time; retailers need to plan how they will bridge the performance gap until the benefits kick in. Without such a plan, investors, the board, and the management team could lose patience fast.

The best tactic for interim survival is to improve operations and get rid of nonessentials in a way that supports longer-term change. Most mature retailers can find considerable savings in their store and administrative costs, in property disposals and sharper stock management, or in both. Moves toward ECR bring additional lasting benefits as they not only cut costs in the short-to-medium term but also support longer-term innovation by putting retailers closer to the consumer. A shrewd survival plan can bring a couple of years' breathing space.

At the same time, the new longer-term strategy needs to be implemented quickly. Don't try to do it all yourself if you don't need to. Outsourcing, acquisitions, or joint ventures can often provide new retail formats or new skills quickly. But retailers still need to be patient—if a concept is really new, it will probably require a lot of fine-tuning. First tries are often disappointing. Retailers should emphasize commitment to steady improvement—not fast results—and keep investors, board members, management, and staff informed of progress.

Coming Back for More

Staying ahead is harder today for mature retailers, but it's not impossible, as Tesco, J.C. Penney, and the new Sears U.S. have proved. Despite their maturity, some older retailers are able to behave like young innovators. They organize for innovation, they learn from setbacks, and they don't give up. Once they're on the comeback trail, mature retailers have an advantage over newcomers: because they've been able to combine an already strong position with new ways of doing business, they're hard to stop.

This article was first published in April 1996.

Richard Lesser and Cynthia R. Cotney

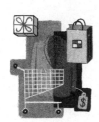

As many companies are discovering, the model of efficient consumer response (ECR) currently in pilot across the grocery industry has not come close to capturing the $30 billion in cost savings that industry experts predicted, let alone to achieving closer partnerships between retailers and suppliers. In fact, many of ECR's early advocates have had mixed results and are reevaluating their approach. We believe the problem is one not of execution but of vision. Too often, ECR implementation focuses on one-size-fits-all logistics platforms and functional linkages. Although this approach can extract some system costs, it fails to provide a growth engine for either partner.

ECR's Mandate

In 1992, an industry group commissioned to document opportunities for cost savings in the U.S. grocery supply chain estimated that $30 billion could be eliminated by cutting systemwide inventory almost in half and improving supply-chain processes. ECR was the road map. Defined as "a collection of many strategies designed to improve value and assortment in the grocery industry based on consumer demands," ECR highlighted four areas for improvement: assortment, replenishment, promotion, and product introductions.

To date, most ECR programs have targeted the replenishment process with systems-based projects aimed at automating store and warehouse logistics. To be sure, these efforts—in some cases long overdue—have produced significant efficiencies across the supply chain, but overall they haven't yet led to savings of the size projected. Even more disappointing, they've failed to stop the grocery industry from losing share to other channels, such as supercenters and discount stores.

One problem with the way ECR has been implemented lies in its narrow focus on areas such as reordering and billing. Although improvements in these areas can have a substantial impact on costs and inventories, the relative advantages are difficult to sustain because they are easily replicated by competitors.

It's not that ECR isn't a good idea. It's just that too few players realize its full potential. One manufacturer noted, "In concentrating on the *efficiency* in ECR, we lost sight of the *consumer*." To get the full benefit from ECR, manufacturers and retailers need to recognize that logistics and operations are only part of a bigger picture. The greater share of ECR's value is still waiting to be unlocked in the other three directions on the road map: store assortment, promotion, and product introduction. It is here that the *C* in ECR comes into play. It is also here that lasting competitive advantage will be found.

Making ECR Work

We believe that capturing the full potential of ECR requires an approach based on five actions. We describe them from a manufacturer's perspective, but the approach applies equally well to retailers.

1. **Set a broader vision.** The goal for you and your ECR partners should be to redefine the value offered to the consumer, not just to improve the supply chain for everyone.

2. **Discover your customers.** Before rushing into systems and operational changes, segment your customers by their capabilities, competitive environment, consumer base, and sources of profitability. Look for potential growth opportunities in their businesses, and determine how you might align your organizations to serve your mutual interests.

3. **Tend to your own garden.** Turn a critical eye on your own operations, products, and organization. Focus not only on internal logistics and information flows but also on those platforms that will help you gain insight into consumers.

4. **Pilot your new capabilities with a small group of high-potential customers.** Get senior management of your company and your ECR partners to agree on joint strategic objectives, identify potential obstacles, and establish ways for the organizations to communicate. Create a process for mutual discovery that will enable each company to understand the other's economics, capabilities, and needs. Establish metrics and measurement processes to capture and evaluate systemwide costs and benefits.

5. **Be prepared to duplicate your success.** Package learning from the pilots in a tool kit of reality-tested solutions that can be customized for other high-potential customers.

One company pursuing this approach is a major food manufacturer. Over the past two years, its management team has focused on efficiency in redesigned business processes as well as on developing tools that realign the supply chain around consumer requirements. This has entailed not only customer service teams, revamped order administration, continuous warehouse replenishment, and shelf-stocking practices but also consumer-based trade management, new planograms, and new products.

The process for introducing these tools has been as important as the tools themselves. The company began by selecting a few customers with which it was able to work to customize the tools. All pilots went well, but the basis for success varied because each customer had a different business model and required different capabilities. In some cases, better trade-promotion management was critical. In others it was dedicated customer service, new planograms, or streamlined logistics. The point is that a one-size-fits-all solution doesn't capture the most important sources of value. But no one can afford (or should want) a customized approach with every customer.

With the initiative now entering its third year, the company is successfully rolling out its new capabilities. As it proceeds, it's creating a growth platform for itself and its best customers.

Changing the Rules of the Game

ECR should be about creating winners and losers. So far, it seems to have created only stalemate. We believe that the chains that define ECR as primarily a logistics solution will ultimately lose. So will the independents and smaller firms that lack the scale to build sufficient infrastructure and consumer insight. Unable to compete with companies that have invested heavily in understanding their customers, they will continue to be swallowed up in successive waves of consolidation. The winners, on the other hand, will have a broader vision of ECR and possess the scale and commitment to make it a reality.

Will the $30 billion ever materialize? No. The original estimates overstated ECR's potential. But real benefits in the billions can be generated. They will go only to the companies that have the strength and imagination to exploit ECR's full potential.

This article was first published in September 1996.

INNER CITIES ARE THE NEXT RETAILING FRONTIER

Michael E. Porter, Mark Blaxill, and Jean Mixer

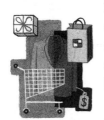

Their earnings growth declining, many U.S. retailers have concluded that the market is saturated and have turned their attentions overseas. And little wonder: with some 19 square feet of retail space per capita—about three times as much as in Europe—the market appears awash in excess capacity. But many U.S. retailers are missing a growth frontier right in their own backyard: the nation's inner cities.

We have conducted a major research effort aimed at examining the retail opportunities in U.S. inner cities—defined as economically distressed communities, in terms of household income, poverty, and unemployment, within a metropolitan area. When we started, we knew the opportunity was large. But we were still surprised by its magnitude.

We estimate that households in U.S. inner cities possess more than $85 billion in annual retail spending power (excluding unrecorded income from legal activities, which could add another $15 billion). That amounts to nearly 7 percent of total U.S. retail spending—far more than Mexico's entire formal retail market.

Inner-city markets are attractive because they are large and densely populated. Despite lower household incomes, inner-city areas concentrate more buying power into a square mile than many affluent suburbs do. But they are badly underserved, often lacking the types of stores that inundate suburban areas—supermarkets, department stores, apparel retailers, and pharmacies, for example. We estimate that today approximately 30 percent, or more than $25 billion, of inner-city retail demand is unmet within the inner city. In some communities, such as Harlem, as much as 60 percent of demand is unmet.

Thus many inner-city residents must travel outside their neighborhoods for the kind of world-class shopping that suburbanites take for granted. Inner-city stores, facing little competition, frequently offer less selection, higher prices, lower quality, inferior customer service, and unappealing ambiance. Our research suggests that inner-city consumers often pay up to 40 percent more than other urban and suburban shoppers pay for basic grocery items. The indignities inner-city consumers endure spending their hard-earned income contribute to the alienation from mainstream America that many feel. One participant in a Harlem focus group was moved to ask, "Is my money a different color, too?"

Our research suggests that retailers' failure to respond to this market opportunity is a matter less of prejudice than of the absence of a strategy. We uncovered a number of challenges in inner cities that can deter market entry. Retailers are concerned about theft and other crime. They also often struggle with regulatory complications, community resistance, and a neglected business infrastructure. Many inner-city neighborhoods are ethnically diverse, each group with its own preferences.

These challenges have led many retailers to conclude that they can't make a profit in the inner city. Yet others have surmounted the challenges. They earn solid profits by simply bringing good retail practices to inner-city neighborhoods.

The moneymaking potential of inner-city retailing may be one of the industry's best-kept secrets. Sears's Boyle Heights store in East Los Angeles is one of the most profitable Sears stores in the region. Ikea's store in Elizabeth, New Jersey, near Newark, is the furniture chain's number one store in North America. Costco's warehouse club in Brooklyn, New York, has been an "above average" performer within the chain since its opening a year ago. Many inner-city supermarkets generate sales per square foot up to 40 percent higher than the regional average. Pathmark stores in Brooklyn's Bedford-Stuyvesant section and Newark's Central Ward, and the Stop & Shop store in Boston's South Bay Center, are all success stories.

Specialty retailers are also thriving. Moo & Oink, a favorite butcher on Chicago's South and West sides, has built a $40 million business offering products like chitterlings (pig intestines) and ham hocks (pig knees) to local residents with Southern tastes. The Lark, a specialty apparel retailer based in Gary, Indiana, operates two profitable inner-city locations that maintain theft rates below the national industry average.

The growth of inner-city retailing is profitable not only for retailers. We estimate that urban developers could generate $500 million in additional rental income from successful inner-city retail corridors. Cities could gain additional tax revenue as well as increase employment and entrepreneurial opportunities for local residents. Filling the unmet inner-city retail demand could create up to 250,000 retail and 50,000 nonretail jobs.

Some retailers have seen this potential and are stepping up plans to open inner-city stores. The Walgreens drug chain indicates that up to 20 percent of new store openings, or up to 100 stores over the next two years, are planned in inner cities. Kmart has created a separate division to focus on urban and inner-city opportunities.

At the same time, many of the historic impediments to doing business in inner cities are falling. Crime rates are dropping and cities such as Indianapolis and Boston are working to reduce regulatory obstacles, improve infrastructure, and spur retail development. The neighborhood business climate is improving as community leaders turn to market-based economic development.

For U.S. retailers, the message should be clear: the nation's inner cities are the next retailing frontier, and they are growing right in their own backyard.

Begin today to target one of the world's largest emerging markets—not China, Indonesia, or Russia but the inner city of the United States. Create the capability to site select, merchandise, promote, recruit, and profit.

Michael E. Porter is a professor of business strategy at Harvard Business School and chairman of the Initiative for a Competitive Inner City.

LEVELS OF THE GAME IN FREQUENCY MARKETING

Tracey Breazeale and Thierry Chassaing

Frequency marketing programs are sweeping the retailing industry. Such programs, when well managed, encourage customers to spend more, more often. Retailers can save on advertising and promotions while they increase the bottom line. Over time, they can enjoy tighter bonds with their customers and can even move them into other, more profitable categories.

Like any new program that seems too good to be true, frequency marketing is not as easy as it looks. Although it's true that many retailers are benefiting from such programs, just as many are going into them with their eyes half shut and their checkbooks wide open. Before embarking on a frequency program, retailers should know how much profit loyal customers are likely to generate, the costs of reaping that profit, the systems they will need, and how they will measure the results.

Unfortunately, there are no standard answers to those questions: different retailing situations call for different programs. However, in working with many kinds of frequency programs over the past several years, we've found it helpful to divide them into three levels of sophistication so that players can assess which program is right for them.

Level 1. Advanced Mass Marketing

Most retailers today haven't moved beyond the basic level of frequency marketing, which we think of as "advanced mass marketing." These retailers have a customer database and are keeping track of basic information. Some may even send out a newsletter or a glossy magazine to all their customers. The typical first-level program rewards customers for cumulative spending. Buy nine cups of coffee, for example, and the tenth is free. In most cases, the free item is one the customer would buy anyway, not a higher-margin product that the retailer might want to introduce—for example, a double latte with a shot of vanilla.

The goal at this level is to increase loyalty and spending, but it's not yet about communicating with individual customers. To move to the next level, retailers should consider marketing that is more targeted. For example, they might offer a free item to customers who fill out a questionnaire about their preferences and shopping habits.

Less than half of retailers make a profit with first-level programs, so many give up. But the problem may be easy to fix. Usually, the retailers have made participation in the program too easy and the rewards too small. As a result, customers have little incentive to remain loyal to the retailer.

Level 2. Targeted Marketing

Retailers who are more sophisticated in using databases can target promotions to specific groups of customers. The goals are to prevent defection, win back customers who have already strayed, and encourage the best customers to shop more often. One retailer, for example, targeted potential defectors by monitoring the use of its proprietary credit card. When a customer's usage dipped, the store would send out a new card or offer a special deal on merchandise the customer regularly purchased. The response rate to this tactic was a surprising 10 percent, and half the respondents became steady customers again.

Successful targeted marketing depends on pinpoint precision—knowing who your best customers are, getting them to shop more frequently, and perhaps even shifting them to other categories with promotions cued to their preferences. But there is no significant decrease in spending on advertising or promotions. Targeted marketing is still more about tactics than about strategy.

Level 3. Organizing Around Customer Segments

At its most sophisticated level, frequency marketing becomes strategic. Here an individual customer's needs drive the introduction of new products and services, and the retailer shifts all the funds that it previously invested in advertising and promotions into the program. Because the retailer knows its customers as individuals, it can tailor offers and communication to create a sense of engagement that competitors cannot begin to imitate.

In addition to "hard" rewards, such as free products, this level also employs "soft" rewards, such as registry programs, personal shoppers, and gift-giving reminders. Such special services and personal attention create long-lasting affiliations by making people feel as though they have a stake in the brand.

Not surprisingly, few retailers have reached this level of marketing, but Neiman Marcus is coming close with its Executive card program. The program starts by giving customers points for purchases, which they can exchange for selected merchandise. Then it encourages high-value customers to shop even more by inviting them to double-point and triple-point shopping nights. The points don't cost the chain much, and the gifts range from as little as .25 percent to 2 percent of sales. Finally, the top tier of shoppers—those who spend $100,000 or more per year—are treated like royalty, with private dressing rooms, special shopping times, personal shoppers, and free tailoring.

Rules of Thumb

Developing a frequency program is a serious undertaking with long-term implications for revenues and funding. For retailers about to step up to the challenge, we offer four rules of thumb:

Start with card-based rewards. The best way to establish a solid customer database—one that tracks at least three-quarters of store sales—is through a card. There are three kinds to consider. The basic version—which is free— simply gives a discount at the cash register. Not surprisingly, it attracts the greatest number of customers, but some people are annoyed at having to enroll in the program to get the discount. Therefore, many retailers have switched to cards that allow customers to accumulate points, which they can redeem for rewards. These cards either are free or require a minimal fee. The third option is a credit card, which provides rich information—such as share of customer wallet—but attracts a smaller number of customers.

Make sure your rewards are the right ones. Whatever the card, you need to offer incentives that will encourage customers to use it often. Safeway supermarkets in Great Britain achieve that by offering customers a multitude of ways to redeem the points they earn from purchases: coupons, "free" products and services, and discounts on travel, insurance policies, and cultural events. Finding the right balance between incentives and their cost is tricky, however. It may require experimenting with different types of incentives to find out which ones appeal to the targeted customer segments and measuring progress against base-line sales. But bear in mind that most start-up programs run close to break-even, at best. Retailers need a substantial sales or margin increase to cover the costs of especially attractive incentives.

Experiment with targeted segments. By focusing on a handful of high-value customers, you can lock in their loyalty and freeze out the competition. But you have to know who your best customers are, what they want, and how to attract more people like them.

Tesco's experimental program in Great Britain works on all those levels. The supermarket chain segments its customers into five groups according to their purchases and sends each group a different version of its *Clubcard* magazine with coupons geared to that group's consumption pattern. Then it tracks customers' purchases by category. The resulting data—such as dietary preferences—enable the store to add personalized vouchers to its quarterly mailings. Once it has identified its highest-spending customers, Tesco invites them—and their friends—to theme shopping evenings, such as a Spanish foods night or a Hawaiian luau. The response rate has been an impressive 70 percent. To graduate to this level of marketing, most retailers will need to redesign their performance measures and acquire more sophisticated IT systems.

Form partnerships with manufacturers. Once retailers have obtained information about their customers, they can pass it on to suppliers in order to help them create more valuable products and more cost-effective promotions. In return, suppliers may be willing to help defray some of the cost of a frequency program. That doesn't mean handing over sensitive data; rather, retailers and suppliers should design promotions and identify targeted segments jointly, on the basis of their understanding of their customers and the product. Retailers, which have more direct and frequent contact with customers, could be particularly helpful to manufacturers, most of which can't afford to target individuals directly.

*   *   *

If you're a retailer and you haven't started a frequency program, you're probably losing share and profits, and you're probably desperate to catch up. But don't let desperation drive your spending. You may need to test several approaches to get the right program, the right rewards, and the right customers.

This article was first published in November 1998.

Anthony Miles and Yves Morieux

Whether they are sales associates, flight attendants, cashiers, hotel receptionists, or telemarketers, frontline employees are central to value creation.

As the first interface with the consumer, they can make or break the relationship. From a strategist's perspective, however, it can be difficult to get frontline employees to treat customers consistently the way the business and the competitive environment demand. Faced with an angry customer, many employees crack: they are either too abrupt, too detached, or only too willing to proffer rebates.

In many cases, such seemingly irrational behavior is a rational attempt to cope with problems that supervisors may not see. To realign frontline behavior with strategic objectives, managers must first understand why employees do what they do. That requires looking behind what they say to the logic revealed by their actions. The key issues to investigate are:

- What is at the root of employees' behavior?

- How does their behavior affect the behavior of other employees?

- How does the combination of behaviors affect the product or service, customer loyalty, and purchase frequency?

The Method in the Madness

Here are some typical behaviors in a variety of operations that contributed to customer dissatisfaction and lost revenues:

- A sales associate in an apparel store kept several customers waiting while she spent an inordinate amount of time trying to help another customer sort through merchandise that the warehouse had mislabeled.

- A cashier in a supermarket responded to complaints about the new check-cashing policy by smiling nicely, handing over the groceries, and saying, "It's not my department."

- The desk clerk at a luxury hotel quickly offered rebates to guests who complained about everything from burned-out light bulbs and dead remote controls to room-service meals that arrived late and rooms that weren't made up promptly.

- The hostess at a popular restaurant regularly turned people away when there were plenty of empty tables.

All those frontline employees were the primary points of contact for customers. They were also part of a constantly changing crew of young people who rarely stayed long enough to earn more than the base wage. Not surprisingly, their organizations concluded that they were to blame for dissatisfied customers.

According to some motivation theories, employees at the bottom of an organization's hierarchy have different needs from employees at the top. Whereas executives seek autonomy and a sense of achievement, clerks supposedly tend to be more interested in wages and a structured, rule-driven environment. Following that reasoning, the managers in the organizations described above put employees through elaborate programs of incentives and attitude training. They offered frontline employees salary increases, schooled them in rules and procedures (down to the detail of how to smile at customers), and, of course, lectured them over and over again about the value of a happy customer. Yet there was little change in their behavior.

The problem, it turns out, wasn't with the frontline employees. It was with the assumption that all they needed was the conventional cocktail of bonuses, training, and rules. The employees had a need all right, but it wasn't to become rich clerks, cashiers, and sales associates. Of course they would have preferred higher compensation, but their most immediate concern—the one that explained their behavior—was to avoid getting put on the spot: pressured, stressed out, and blamed for problems over which they had no control. And the employees were using the resources they had available to do just that.

The sales associate's strategy was to overcompensate for the warehouse's poor performance by leaving her station to search for mislabeled merchandise. She satisfied the complaining customer but not the ones waiting in line. The most common result of such overcompensation, not surprisingly, is burnout—which can lead to high turnover. Contrary to what many believe, employees don't quit their jobs because they are young and inexperienced but because they get tired of making up for deficiencies in the business system.

Another coping strategy is to hide behind the rules. It's not that frontline employees are particularly fond of rules, but they may have few other resources available to protect them from customer pressure. Smiling nicely at the frustrated shopper, the supermarket cashier announced that he wasn't able to help. Smiling nicely at the angry hotel guest, the desk clerk explained that she wasn't responsible and offered a rebate. Unfortunately, such giveaways rarely brought guests back for a return visit.

A third strategy is to manipulate the rules—in the hostess's case, the seating system. As sometimes happens at restaurants, relations between the "front of the house" and the kitchen staff were strained. Knowing that a full restaurant would increase tension and result in poor service—for which she and the wait staff would be blamed—the hostess made sure the restaurant was never booked to capacity.

Whether it is overcompensation, weak apologies and rebates, or manipulating the rules, the aggregated effect of frontline coping behaviors can be unused capacity, high employee turnover, declining customer loyalty, lower revenues, and a reputation for service excellence lost to the competition.

Getting the Right Power to the Right People

Instead of trying to persuade people to change their behavior, it is far more effective first to understand why they behave as they do and then to adjust what drives their actions. Usually the answer isn't more motivational speeches, nor is it further investment in customer-interface training. Instead of focusing only on frontline employees, managers need to look across interdependent groups, not just to ensure consistent training and compensation but also to distribute power and responsibility appropriately.

Once management has a detailed picture of the organization's behavioral dynamics—the resources and constraints that determine frontline employees' behavior given the challenges they face—the next step is to change those dynamics. For instance, the people behind the frontline need to feel the cost of dissatisfied customers so that frontline employees—the lightning rods for customer complaints—can depend on their prompt response.

Sometimes better cooperation among departments can be accomplished with new role definitions, career tracks, and performance measures. Sales associates and inventory clerks, for example, might be given the same position in the hierarchy, and employees could rotate from one department to another to understand how all departments work together.

An organization might also overlap responsibilities or include frontline employees in strategic decisions in order to encourage teamwork. If a store's managers are going to change the check-cashing policy, for instance, they must anticipate how the change could affect the relationship between cashiers and customers. They may decide to bring other people forward to explain the changes and handle complaints. Finally, frontline employees should contribute to their colleagues' performance evaluations, which would give them some leverage over the people they depend on to help customers.

Demystifying Behavior

If the behavior of your frontline employees is not satisfying customers, look beyond what they are doing to the context in which they are operating. Here are four steps that will help you understand the method behind what may seem to be madness.

1. Single out the people who are directly and indirectly involved in satisfying customers. What value do they add to the product or service? What other functions must they depend on? What challenges do they face in performing their roles?

2. List each person's resources and constraints. Those could include skills, information, rules, and authority lines (or lack thereof), as well as people with conflicting interests.

3. Identify the behaviors or coping strategies that employees adopt to deal with their challenges in light of their resources and constraints, and compare those behaviors with what they should be. To change behavior, you need to change the resources or constraints; exhortation alone is never enough.

4. Draw up a series of scenarios in which different challenges, resources, or constraints would lead a frontline employee to adopt the desired behavior. One scenario might modify a challenge by changing the employee's role and position. Another might modify both constraints and challenges by altering evaluation criteria and career paths. Yet another might make certain resources—such as skills, information, or reporting lines—more accessible or might eliminate a constraint, such as a particular metric or procedure.

With appropriate tools and the same objective and analytical rigor used in other business situations, managers can uncover the missing link between a company's strategy and its implementation at the frontline. When that happens, people are engaged, personal strategies line up behind business strategies, and enormous value is created for the organization and its people.

This article was first published in February 1999.

Matthew A. Krentz and Kevin Waddell

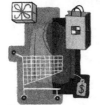

Creating shareholder value has been a frustrating challenge for retailers. Over the past ten years, retailers have pursued growth opportunities aggressively. Yet despite a few well-known success stories—Wal-Mart, the Gap, Home Depot—retail equities as a group have lagged behind the stock market. In contrast, consumer goods manufacturers considerably outperformed the market during the late 1980s and have matched it during the 1990s (see Exhibit 8). For retailers to systematically earn high returns, they must shift from a tactical focus on operations to a more strategic focus on value creation. For many, this will require new metrics for their businesses.

Choosing the Right Metrics

In the past decade, many retailers developed complex product lines, formats, and portfolio mixes in the belief that growth would follow and would create value. But when growth didn't materialize, the retailers turned their attention to day-to-day operations. Consequently, the growth opportunities they did pursue tended to be incremental.

The metrics that retailers used to measure their performance heightened this focus on short-term, incremental opportunities. Consider two of the most common measures: gross margin and sales per square foot. Although useful for determining near-term operating performance, they reveal very little about critical value drivers, such as growth, profitability, and capital efficiency. In fact, gross margin doesn't show product, segment or business profitablity, it is one of the *least* useful measures in retailing.

In contrast, consider a broader measure, such as cash flow return on investment (CFROI). In addition to accounting for margins, CFROI also reveals asset characteristics, turnover, and other factors that affect business performance. CFROI can help managers determine strategic direction and allocate resources across a portfolio of businesses, but it can also be used to drill down into an individual business to identify the investments that are earning above or below the cost of the capital.

Exhibit 8

Retailers Have Lagged Behind Consumer Goods Companies and the Stock Market

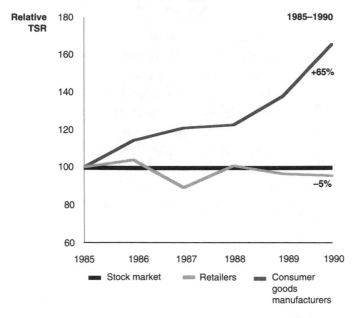

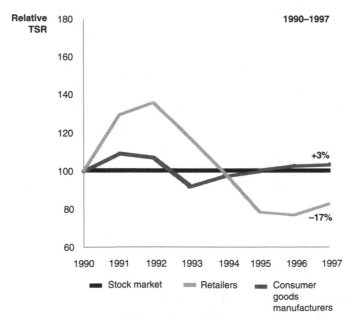

The graphs show the total shareholder returns (TSR is defined as capital gains plus reinvested dividends) of the retail and consumer goods industries in relation to the stock market. (The market TSR is indexed to 100.) From 1985 to 1997, consumer goods outperformed the market by 68 points—driven almost entirely by the performance from 1985 to 1990—while retailers underperformed by 22 points.

Linking Performance to Shareholder Value

Earning high returns, and thus creating value for shareholders, usually depends on three activities: growing successful businesses, inventing concepts or categories that provide high returns and are hard to copy, and improving or divesting weak businesses. Wal-Mart and Sears provide real-world examples. Wal-Mart grew its discount retail business aggressively during the 1980s, increasing the number of stores from 230 in 1979 to more than 1,300 in 1989. The company created enormous value for shareholders in the process. But when the concept of discount retailing matured in the early 1990s and growth slowed, shareholder value flattened. Wal-Mart responded by adding supermarkets to its general merchandise stores, and returns and stock prices started to rise again.

Sears faced an entirely different situation. Diversification and the emergence of new comptitors (Wal-Mart and specialty stores) weakened some of its businesses. Sears exited a few of them—most notably, it closed the catalog operation in 1993—and spun off others. This allowed it to focus on fixing the store's core retail business by developing the highly profitable "softer side" in apparel.

Wal-Mart and Sears didn't necessarily use CFROI, but they did focus on their most successful businesses, they invested in categories that would provide high returns, and they got rid of weak performers. Those are activities that CFROI pushes companies to pursue.

In addition to measuring return on investment, CFROI can also be applied to more tactical issues within a business. We recently calculated the CFROI for each store within a retail client's local markets (see Exhibit 9). No surprises there. The analysis confirmed the retailer's suspicions about which stores were strong and which were weak. But when we linked a store's performance to shareholder value, the real power of methodology emerged. Several of the underperformers did much worse in terms of actual cash flow and shareholder value than the retailer had believed.

That perspective forced the company to consider store investments in a new light. Before, the retailer had taken a strictly incremental view: if a new project—say, a store renovation—was estimated to have a positive net present value (NPV), the retailer would make the investment. What NPV fails to measure, however, is whether an investment has paid off. The renovated store, for example, might still be returning below the cost of capital, and its market value might not be improved. In other words, the investment did not deliver value to the shareholders. CFROI changed the retailer's judgment about which stores to operate and which to shut down. Once the com-

Exhibit 9

CFROI Highlighted True Economic
Performance at the Store Level

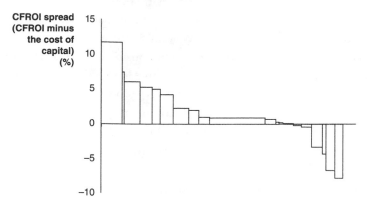

The chart shows the CFROI for individual stores in a local market as a function of gross investment for each store. The width of each bar indicates the level of gross investment in that particular store.

pany saw how some stores were damaging the overall value of the business (in dollars per share), it was ready to take the unpleasant but necessary steps it had been avoiding.

Drilling even deeper into the retailer's businesses, we applied a similar approach to its merchandise categories. We looked at each category's CFROI and at its growth in investment (see Exhibit 10). We found little relationship between the two, which meant that the retailer was neither identifying growth opportunities for high-return categories nor fixing or exiting low-return categories. As a result of our finding, the retailer now requires demonstrated returns above the cost of capital before approving investments. And it is also looking more closely at the strategic issues within its portfolio: which categories are core to the business and how to increase their value, the costs of keeping underperforming categories, and what new categories might be worth entering.

Delivering Shareholder Value

To make the right strategic and portfolio decisions day to day, retailers must link operating and performance metrics to the creation of shareholder value. CFROI is one of the best measures for helping them achieve this objective. General and line managers could be evaluated on CFROI performance, while employees could be evaluated on one component of CFROI, such as sales, customer returns, or inventory turns. CFROI as a single, all-encompassing

Exhibit 10

Category Investments Were Not Linked to Profitability

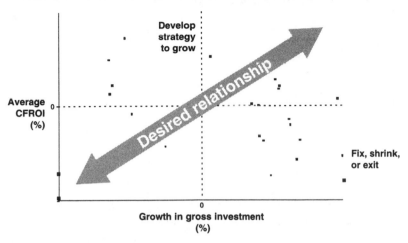

The matrix contrasts the CFROI of different merchandise categories (represented by the points on the graph) with the growth of the gross investment in each category.

value-based metric can also help motivate a change in strategy. One retailer recently described it this way: "We were too focused on net income. When we began concentrating on cash flow and the balance sheet, people saw specific things they could do to unlock value, such as increasing margins, speeding up processes, and reducing investments. People were able to understand the impact of their efforts on CFROI and, ultimately, on shareholder value."

For the past two decades, retailers have failed to deliver the value that shareholders expect. In light of the overcapacity in the industry, the low barriers to entry, and the ease with which new concepts can be replicated by competitors, reversing that trend will require new strategic frameworks and competitive levers. Retailers must reevaluate their portfolios throughthe critical lens of shareholder value. They must grow high-return businesses, fix or divest underperformers, and develop the high performers of tomorrow. And to make sure that tough, value-based decisions bear fruit, retailers must link daily operations to value-based metrics.

This article was first published in April 1999.

Part Three

MARKETING AND SELLING

FROM LONE RANGERS
TO THE NEW SELLING ELITE

Carlos Costa, Lindy Hirschsohn, and Anthony Pralle

A revolution is rapidly transforming nearly every aspect of sales. This revolution uses science and analysis to generate share gain, primary demand growth, and improved margins. It is exhilarating for the new selling elite and daunting for salespeople still approaching their clients the old-fashioned way, with a sample pack, price list, and order form.

Recently, a national retailer called its category vendors in for a business review. One large company brought samples of new products. A second vendor outlined its coupon and trade-deal programs. A third vendor presented a comprehensive report, including

- an analysis of in-store conditions based on the demographics (population, lifestyles, buying patterns) of different geographic locations

- recommendations for pricing based on an understanding of elasticity

- a new, larger in-store hardware set that provided consumers with information, promotional excitement, and easy shopping

- a "guarantee" of improved profitability based on a refined product mix, store-by-store revenue projections, and reallocation of the profit pool to the advantage of the retailer and the aligned vendor

The retailer CEO responded immediately, "That's what we want. Let's do it!"

Since the meeting, the stores have been reset, the pricing has been redone, and the aligned vendor has doubled its profitability. The other vendors have suffered a rapid decline, and they don't know why.

Information and Solution Providers

This radical transformation of the traditional sales process is not just on the horizon; it is happening now. Today, leading companies are redefining brands to encompass not just the product, or even its image, but the *total customer experience*—from purchase to use to after-sales service. Sales teams will be playing a starring role in that experience. Instead of being a pipeline through which to push products, they will be seen—and see themselves—

as information and solution providers. Today's world-class sales teams don't just sell products, they provide consumers with solid evidence that the brand adds the value they are looking for.

Consider the case of a yellow-pages publisher suffering from high customer attrition and stagnant sales. It discovered that while its customers considered product quality to be adequate, they rated the company low for its inability to provide quantitative proof that their advertising dollars were being well spent. What's more, it turned out that this information was more important to customers' purchase decisions than the product itself. With nothing to convince them that yellow-pages listings were more effective in attracting profitable business than other media, it's no wonder that customers regularly drifted away.

The revelation that its customers expected to be offered economic insights as well as an ad listing led the yellow-pages company to revamp its underskilled work force. The result was a completely new learning program designed around customers' expectations.

Instead of the traditional two-week "sales training," followed by sink-or-swim immersion in the field, the company established an apprenticeship model for continuous learning and improvement. The program extended over a year and focused on "just in time" learning. Classroom study was reinforced through fieldwork practice with coaches. Finally, a sequence of certification hurdles ensured that salespeople had mastered high performance levels in specific skills.

For the first time, yellow-pages sales recruits were exposed to customer-account segmentation, basic financial analysis, and the use of database tracking tools. Customer "report cards" were introduced to encourage customer-specific action plans, targeted feedback from supervisors, and information sharing among peers.

Supervisors were also given a new mandate. No longer administrators, they had to be reeducated for a new leadership role, which required stronger analytic skills and significantly more hands-on coaching.

The New Sales Teams

Other companies are beginning to discover the need for a radically upgraded sales force to serve increasingly sophisticated customers. But product pushers can't be transformed into insight generators overnight. It takes an initial investment in recruiting, training, and technology, as well as a fully committed customer-focused organization. Here are two additional strategies that the front-runners are employing:

Pumping up while slimming down. Most sales forces have been downsized to match consolidated markets, concentrated channels, and automated ordering. To be sure, these efficiencies have resulted in real savings, but some companies are beginning to find themselves overmatched by competitors that have invested in building up their sales capabilities.

To keep salespeople at top productivity, leading companies are putting money back into information technology systems that will help leaner sales forces control customer densities, manage sales routes, and identify the most profitable accounts. They are also using formal evaluation and incentive systems to increase productivity and achieve longer-term, account-focused relationships. Such relationships free up the sales force to concentrate on the kinds of information, insights, and influence that will be most valuable to customers and provide long-term rewards for the investment.

Integrating lone rangers into service teams. Of course, there have always been "born" salespeople who had exceptional insight into customers' needs and offered value beyond the product. But there aren't enough of these "naturals" to go around. Today's marketplace demands whole teams of highly skilled and dedicated people in sales, marketing, logistics, and IT to manage the myriad customer contacts for maximum brand strength. The traditional lone ranger could neither identify nor deliver solutions for most customer problems today.

One service company, for example, gives its sales team the tools to calculate each customer's economic situation: how much the customer was spending on various cleaning options; where he or she could save money and labor by switching products or using them in a different way; and how he or she could better track and control product use. Today the company has no doubt that its ability to provide economic insights as well as solutions to specific product problems has greatly increased net profits, while customer retention is at an all-time high.

Preparing for the New Sales Teams

As products get better, it's harder to differentiate them on quality alone. Therefore, advantage is being sought further down the value chain in the customer relationship. To work at this level, the whole organization must be transformed into a sales team whose greatest competitive tools are the service it gives its customers and its focus on the bottom line. That requires investing in the best salespeople, training them continually, and managing them to work in teams where intelligence and creativity are encouraged. Ask yourself the following questions about your organization:

- Does our sales force consistently deliver insight and competitive intelligence?

- Are salespeople from other companies trying to join our organization?

- Is our field force better today than it was five years ago? Do we have a plan to make it better five years from now?

- Is the compensation of our sales force aligned with our company's long-term profit goals?

- Do we have a chance to leapfrog a competitor on the basis of better knowledge, better analysis, or a more creative solution?

If you can't answer a resounding "yes" to every question, you could be caught unprepared when the sales renaissance comes to your industry.

This article was first published in May 1996.

THE RESEARCH ADVANTAGE:
THE MARKETPLACE MEETS MANAGEMENT

Jeannine Bergers Everett

How would you describe your market research organization? Is it the department that collects data? Manages research projects? Provides critical numbers? Are you concerned about research costs? Have you outsourced more responsibility to vendors or cut research staff? Instead of questioning the amount you invest in research, maybe you should ask if your research organization is structured to deliver true strategic value.

The role of research has always been to speak for the consumer. Today, when the consumer's experience with the brand is the primary source of competitive differentiation and advantage, understanding the consumer must be at the core of a company's strategy. For this to happen, a number of traditional research practices will have to change.

Making Research Strategic

Transforming a traditional market-research organization into a strategic team takes time, commitment, and something researchers are particularly good at: research. The first task is to understand the current impact of research on business decisions, the costs involved, and whether recommendations are followed.

Research departments typically operate in one of four ways. Below we characterize them, identify the key deficiency of each style, and describe some corrective actions. How much does your organization resemble these models?

Explorers. Their research assignments don't seem to have a specific purpose. No business decision is directly related to their work, and therefore no recommendations for action are made. Considerable money may be spent on research, but no one knows where it goes. The solution? Reconnect the research department's understanding of consumers to the business's strategic needs.

Order Takers. They play a role in the business but not in the decision-making process. Management defines the issue and requests a specific study. The reports present consumer data but make no specific recommendations for action. Indeed, researchers rarely learn what actions are eventually taken. Research is evaluated on cost and timing, not strategic input. In this situation, researchers need to begin a dialogue with senior management while they develop the skills to move to the next level.

Silent Advisers. They are directed toward decision-making but have little voice in the process. Senior managers believe research is important, but they don't think the department itself belongs in strategic decisions. The challenge for research here is to identify the credibility gap and reposition itself as a value-added partner in the business.

Consumer Advocates. They are highly integrated into business decisions. They decide when and if research is necessary while leveraging their understanding of consumers and their business knowledge across a range of decisions. Research is viewed not as a cost center for data provision but as an investment in understanding the consumer. Consumer advocates don't necessarily spend more on research; they do, however, tend to spend their research money more wisely, since they know where it is going. Here the task is to leverage a superior understanding of the consumer to build marketplace dominance.

Finding Consumer Advocates

It takes dedicated consumer advocates to develop an advocate organization. These people have a special ability to understand the consumer and to make the most of their insights. These are their main characteristics:

- Advocates are strategists who happen to have highly developed technical skills. They are dedicated to research as a career choice but are driven primarily by their interest in exploring consumer behavior, not by their love of technique. For them, statistics and research tools are a means to an end, not the end in itself.

- Advocates are insatiably curious about consumers. To anticipate consumer needs and desires, they go beyond the obvious questions; they look for the deeper motivations at play. They constantly scan the horizon to catch the innovation curve in its infancy—or even to create it.

- Advocates talk constantly with consumers. They view projects not as disparate individual studies but as a series of snapshots that, intelligently organized, paint a multidimensional portrait of the consumer.

- Finally, advocates don't live in ivory towers. They speak out for consumers in daily business decisions. They play a critical role within the organization. They understand that information creates power only if it is shared. They encourage, and sometimes even force, management to meet consumers and become actively involved in the research process.

Reviving Your Research Department

Could you transform your research department into a consumer advocate operation? One consumer products company that The Boston Consulting Group worked with decided to do just that. Its research was strong, but the company lagged in the marketplace. A decision audit revealed that the researchers were operating as Silent Advisers—providing solid information but with little impact. Despite the company's belief that it had world-class research, research results were not connected to business decisions. The reporting process was lengthy and formal, which often meant that results were too late to be useful or that actions were poorly articulated.

The solution was an informal, high-involvement approach to ensure that results were clearly communicated and incorporated into market plans. For the next brand launch, management and the research department assembled a multidisciplinary team—a company within the company—whose task was to move the brand from the concept to the shelf. Brand development still relied heavily on consumer research, but the team used a different communication model to speed up the process.

As results came in, the team discussed them in a relaxed setting, with the research department facilitating the conversation. That effectively collapsed the time-consuming process of writing, approving, releasing, transporting, reading, evaluating, and discussing the research into a record-breaking single meeting. Decisions were made and implemented immediately. Instead of being a detailed presentation of findings, the report to senior management simply documented what was discussed and agreed to.

This new approach allowed the company to launch a brand that would become the most successful in its history—in half the time it typically took for brand development. The process was so successful that it eventually became the operating model for the entire organization.

Building a Consumer Advocate Organization

As the example indicates, transforming the research department is only half the battle. The organizational culture and structure must also change to capitalize on the power and insight that advocate research can create.

For an organization to reap the benefits of consumer advocacy, research must have a voice in decision-making beyond findings or reports. It means daily interactions providing the consumer's viewpoint across a range of disciplines and activities. It also means that advocates need to know the concerns of the business and where it is heading.

Integrating research into business decisions will also require organizational support. Lines of responsibility and influence should be clear so that every decision-maker knows who the consumer advocate is. This creates a research organization that mirrors the organization as a whole, rather than an adjunct department divided by research techniques or a flexible pool with random work assignments.

Finally, too many "partner" relationships focus on moving research activities outside the organization. External research vendors can be important in dealing with increasing budgets and decreasing staff. They cannot, however, provide the daily participation in business decisions of an internal market-research department.

What's Your Status?

Do you have a consumer advocate organization? Answering these questions may help you find out.

- What is the role of market research?

- How involved is research in the day-to-day operation of the business?

- How well does research evaluate the business risk of decisions?

- How well does research identify business opportunities on the basis of consumer insight and marketplace trends?

- Does research recommend actions on the basis of its findings? How appropriate are those actions?

Becoming a consumer advocate organization takes work, and today there are fewer people to do it. Focusing on research that matters, however, frees time from research that doesn't. The days of fruitlessly hunting through reams of data and generating lengthy tomes that no one reads are over. Zeroing in on key decisions helps to deliver the required insight quickly, efficiently, and intelligently. Research can be more than just the center for data collection. It should be the company's most critical strategic link between the marketplace and management.

This article was first published in October 1997.

GIVE US YOUR TIRED, YOUR POOR, YOUR NEGLECTED CUSTOMERS

Dean Nelson

If you've raised prices and lowered costs as far as they can go, you're probably looking to growth to sustain and expand profits. Typically, that  means going after your competitor's market share. Victory, however, is often expensive, and maintaining advantage is a constant battle.

A few organizations are moving beyond these territorial skirmishes, and we think they're onto something. These companies are growing by entering markets no one else wants: the neglected segments of underserved, geographically remote, or poorly regarded customers.

To reach these new markets, pioneering companies are acting as agents or orchestrators. *Agents* help customers find the products or services they've been missing. *Orchestrators* focus on the product or service features that customers care most about and outsource the rest. Significantly, both types of companies have invested heavily in consumer databases—an advantage that makes it nearly impossible for competitors to catch up.

The Agent's Advantage

1-800-FLOWERS, the gift-giving service, is a classic example of the agent model. It reminds customers of their personal gift-giving occasions, tells them what they gave before, and prompts them to take timely action by offering a range of products for the next gift. The service succeeded because it didn't have to fight off established competitors. No one else had thought about how to use technology to reach these consumers—workaholics too busy to shop for gifts and too harried to remember anniversaries and birthdays.

But it's not just affluent consumers who offer potential. One company has had remarkable success with a segment that is both remote and budget-conscious, and therefore perceived as unprofitable: small-town U.S.A.

This player sought its unpopular market in an even more unpopular industry: movie theaters. Ten years ago, their prognosis was pretty dismal. Attendance was nearly stagnant, earnings were sinking, and VCRs and cable TV were gaining ground. For small-town theaters, in particular, it looked like the last picture show. These single-screen operations were typically large old theaters with outdated facilities and equipment. Worse, they often ran a single movie for as long as a month. Even the multiplex operators couldn't see a way to make them profitable.

Enter Carmike Cinemas. Instead of a dying market, the company saw legions of forgotten citizens starving for entertainment. Ignoring industry wisdom, which decrees that you need a base population of a quarter of a million to support a multiplex, Carmike proceeded to build 10- to 15-screen palaces in towns one-fifth that size. The economics worked, despite a penetration that was five times that in big cities. Lower revenues per screen were more than compensated for by higher revenues per location, thanks to imaginative promotions and improved concession-stand operations. Inexpensive real estate and careful staff scheduling also helped to lower operating costs.

Carmike now controls more movie screens in the U.S. than any other theater operator, with 60 percent of its capacity in monopoly markets. This, in turn, gives it tremendous leverage with distributors, which it has used not to lower costs but to demand the variety its customers had been lacking. And because Carmike is the only game in many towns, it can get new movies with much shorter booking times, which brings in more and more customers.

Carmike designed an information system to run the theaters. Called IQ Zero, the system controls bookings, show times, and scheduling, and even tracks concession revenues down to the last gumdrop. More important, it measures customer response to different shows and schedules. With the ability to analyze local demographics against type of film, run length, and featured stars, Carmike has become better at predicting blockbusters than most filmmakers.

Operating with less than half of what traditional theaters spend, Carmike has achieved earnings 7 percentage points higher than the rest of the industry. Its growth rate has been 25 percent over the past decade, and its stock has outperformed the industry average.

How did Carmike do it? It looked at what customers weren't getting and then provided it. In this case, it was greater variety in a better environment. But the source of Carmike's sustainable advantage is that it forestalled its competition by quickly acquiring a dominant, unassailable position, which provided leverage with distributors. Finally, by telling producers what customers wanted to see and then bringing those neglected customers the films they wanted, Carmike has become an agent to both ends of the value chain.

Orchestrator for the Overlooked

As skilled outsourcers, orchestrators too can enter new businesses rapidly, despite limited assets. That's how Jim Koch was able to start Boston Beer.

Until 1990, the domestic market for high-end beer in North America was practically nonexistent. The rare beer drinker who insisted on quality was pretty much limited to a few expensive imports.

Determined to start a microbrewery using his grandfather's recipe, Koch asked himself what this small, neglected segment of beer connoisseurs cared about most. The answer, of course, was taste. To get that, Koch realized, he needed an outstanding recipe, excellent ingredients, controlled brewing, and a way to deliver the beer while it was still fresh. (Imported beer was vulnerable on freshness because of complicated distribution channels involving transatlantic travel.)

Koch had the recipe, but he didn't own a brewery. With excess capacity in the U.S. brewing industry, however, he got rates from existing breweries that were $20 per barrel less than integrated breweries spent.

Today, 90 percent of the company's total volume comes from contract breweries. This allows Koch to concentrate on quality control, which has two basic elements: managing the ingredients and monitoring the product. It also requires a strong purchasing department and a rigorous inspection department.

As an orchestrator of his own value chain, Koch has three big advantages: his customers get a quality product; the company has been able to grow much faster than competitors in its market segment; and, because the product enjoys a premium price, distributors and retailers make higher profits, which keeps them loyal.

Do customers mind that Boston Beer isn't brewed in Boston? "If Julia Child brings her own recipe and ingredients into someone else's kitchen and cooks a meal," Koch asks, "isn't it still Julia Child who is making the meal?"

Boston Beer costs nearly twice as much to produce as regular beer, but its operating profits are nearly twice the industry average. Distributors make two and a half times as much on a case of Boston Beer, and retailers make twice as much. Everyone in the value chain benefits.

Companies like 1-800-FLOWERS, Carmike, and Boston Beer refuse to see the market as a zero-sum game. They don't want to fight wars of attrition, customer by customer. To determine whether your company could profit from being an agent or an orchestrator, consider these questions:

1.   Who are the neglected customers in my industry?

2.   What can I offer these customers that no one has offered them before?

3.   What parts of the value chain matter most to these customers?

4.   What information technology tools will I need in order to succeed quickly as an agent or an orchestrator?

This article was first published in February 1998.

Felix Barber

Let your food be your medicine, and your medicine be your food.

—Hippocrates

John and Jane Collins are preparing dinner after a busy day at the office. It will *take less than five minutes. From the freezer, John, 52, chooses one of four meals*  *designed to control his cholesterol, limit his calorie intake, and guar-* *antee a good night's sleep. Jane, 47, selects an entrée that helps her* *maintain her 1,200-calorie-a-day diet and includes supplements* *to combat anemia, osteoporosis, memory loss, and low blood pres-* *sure. For dessert, they share a "healthy-fat" strawberry cheesecake* *containing antioxidants, which capture free radicals in the blood-* *stream and help prevent cancer. Since John started his diet, his stamina is up and* *his pulse rate is down. Jane has more energy and reports that she no longer feels hungry* *all the time.*

This scene may sound futuristic, but it's not science fiction. Food manufacturers are rapidly developing the ability to design products that help prevent specific diseases, increase longevity, and reduce health care costs. Early launches include ConAgra's Advantage/10, a 14-SKU line of natural foods endorsed by a well-known physician, and Ross Labs' liquid-diet brand Ensure, which enjoys $500 million in sales. Even companies not usually associated with health are introducing nutrition products: witness Coca-Cola's Fruitopia vitamin drinks and, in Germany, Haribo's Pep-Up fruit chewing gums.

These companies and others are setting their sights on the huge market of consumers who believe that a better diet can help them live longer and healthier lives. Why is this happening now? In part because the diseases that preoccupy the aging population in most of the developed world—heart disease, cancer, and arthritis—have proved intractable to conventional medicine. Faced with increasing evidence that those diseases are related to lifestyle, people are taking health management into their own hands by controlling what they consume, what they do, and where they do it. Health care is moving out of the doctor's office and into the kitchen, the smoke-free restaurant, and the exercise club.

This trend presents enormous opportunities for the food, fitness, and pharmaceutical industries. According to Stephen Felice, president of the Foundation for Innovation in Medicine, so-called nutraceuticals could become a $250 billion market in the United States. Nutraceuticals include vitamin and mineral supplements, foods that fight specific diseases, low-fat foods, and "good for you" products such as fruit juices with added calcium. The variety of products in this market may increase further through the use of genetic engineering. The pharmaceutical company Zeneca, for example, is already working on genetically engineered tomatoes that contain more lycopene—a chemical that may reduce the risk of prostate and other cancers—than ordinary tomatoes.

Scores of established companies—including Quaker, ConAgra, Heinz, American Home Products, Monsanto, General Nutrition, Nestlé, and Novartis—have invested in health-related brands and businesses. As more companies follow suit over the next decade, the entire food industry is likely to be transformed. Many of today's best-selling products will go into decline, and fortunes will be made with the health-oriented products that replace them.

To assess how this new market will affect your company and to create new business opportunities, you first need to explore which of the many customer segments you want to serve. Once you've identified promising ones, you'll need to develop a strategy for breaking the tough compromises you'll encounter in marketing to them.

Understanding Health-Market Segmentation

Whatever your market focus, you should consider the full range of health-market options to avoid being blind-sided. Health-market segmentation is complex, and it cuts across traditional food and beverage segments.

First, the health theme lets companies link a hitherto largely self-contained food and beverage market to other categories of consumer goods and services. That is what Heinz did when it acquired the Weight Watchers clubs and introduced diet-food products under that brand. And it is what Kanebo, the Japanese cosmetics company, did when it put its brand on a diet drink containing aloe vera and silk traces. Second, a wide range of neutral, or even "sinful," foods could become "healthy" with the addition of certain ingredients, such as Procter & Gamble's fat substitute Olestra. Third, as medical research continues to find new connections between diet and disease, food and beverage marketers receive a steady stream of new health-marketing challenges. The recently confirmed link between meat consumption and cancer, for example, creates interesting opportunities for companies to market foods made from vegetable proteins.

Understanding the health market is a daunting task, but it will help your company uncover ways to defend its existing business as well as provide new opportunities. Once you've chosen your areas of focus, however, the hard part begins, because you still have a number of compromises to negotiate.

Natural *and* High Tech?

Consumers are looking for products that are at once natural and high tech, although those qualities seem to be mutually exclusive. In fact, some companies have learned that you can have it both ways. Nestlé's LC1 probiotic yogurt, for example, is a high tech product that is being marketed as natural; and the Swiss Coop's NATURAplan brand of produce is a natural product that uses technology in its organic processing. Both appeal to the natural-food segment of the market while using sophisticated technology to enhance their "natural" qualities.

Hard Health Claims *and* Low Costs?

Products that claim to fight specific diseases are fueling the health market's growth, but without the clinical trials required for regulatory approval, such claims can only be hinted at. Yet the high costs of clinical trials may be hard to justify if the product must compete with a prescription drug covered by insurance.

Fortunately, most consumers believe that health is more important than money. That is why Benecol, for example, a cholesterol-reducing margarine made by the Finnish company Raisio, can sell for seven times the price of conventional margarine. Still, companies are sometimes constrained in how much they can charge for products with well-established health claims and must settle for relatively low margins. One way around that constraint may be to increase volume so that production costs will fall and R&D expenses can be amortized. Not surprisingly, Raisio recently announced a global marketing alliance with Johnson & Johnson to leverage its Scandinavian franchise.

Product Breadth with Product Competence?

Health products aren't limited to foods and beverages. They also include skin and hair creams, sports clothing and equipment, and services such as diet plans. The U.K. retailer Boots the Chemist has a broad health-care image and has put together a variety of health products, including health insurance, under the Boots brand. Often, however, even if a brand will stretch, a company's product and channel capabilities may not. To exploit their opportunities fully, food manufacturers may need to team up with partners that have complementary product-development or branding competence.

New Brand Image with Traditional Brand Franchise?

Piggybacking a new health product onto an existing brand will lower both costs and risks. If the product is complementary, one brand could encompass both products: witness Coca-Cola's success in changing Tab's name to Diet Coke or Coke Light. If the product is an ingredient in other products, its brand name could appear on the host product's label, as the sweetener Xylitol's does on the label of the chewing gum Stimorol. But if the new product's image conflicts with the brand, another brand may have to be created, as Guinness has done with its nonalcoholic beer, Kaliber.

Specialist-Channel Credibility with Mass-Market Volume?

Historically, nutrition products have had their own distribution channels. These now include retailers—such as General Nutrition, Whole Foods Market, and Great Earth in the U.S., and the Reformhäuser in Germany; and nutrition services—such as virtual stores on the Web, including The Zone and Mother Nature's General Store. The rapidly growing specialist channels have considerable credibility and contribute generous margins, and their informed salespeople can support new product launches. But they aren't for everyone. Companies with mass-market products will find that only the mainstream food and drug channels offer the margins and volumes they require.

Some products that used specialist channels during the launch phase, however—among them Celestial Seasonings teas—have held on to their cachet long after entering mainstream distribution. Given their success, more specialist-channel products are likely to try to cross over to the mass market.

In view of the challenging compromises in the business system and considerable marketing uncertainty, formulating a health strategy will not be easy. Nevertheless, as the scientific evidence linking health with diet and lifestyle continues to mount, health-related products will constitute a huge new market. No matter what kinds of products and services your company offers, whether you're a manufacturer or a retailer, consider the opportunities that consumers like John and Jane Collins present. Your company's health could be at stake.

This article was first published in July 1998.

Part Four

THE CONSUMER

Jeannine Bergers Everett and Philip Siegel

Good innovators have double vision. They are dreamers with an eye on reality, and realists who dream of what could be. Market segmentation is a critical tool for helping innovators understand *what is*, but too often it prevents them from exploring *what could be*. Here are three rules that innovators use to keep from falling into segmenting traps:

1. **Segment consumers, not the product portfolio.** If, for example, you see your segments as cars and vans, what do you do with people who own both? Or people who may buy the same product, but for different reasons and in different channels? Or someone who wants something altogether different from what you offer? Thinking only in terms of trucks, vans, and cars, for example, caused many automakers to miss the innovation of the minivan, the jeep, and the roadster.

2. **Look beyond the product to the need it fulfills.** Segmenters often get distracted by product features and miss the larger purpose the product serves. People don't eat cereal, for instance; they eat breakfast. This means that if your focus is only on cereal, you're missing the boat. Much of the competition for cold cereal is indeed coming from private-label products, but fast-growing breakfast alternatives outside the cereal category, such as bagels, toaster pastries, and breakfast bars, pose an equal threat. Beverage companies refer to this concept as "share of throat"; bankers, as "share of wallet."

3. **Appreciate consumers' complex lives.** Consumers are multifaceted. Yet segmenters tend to focus on one dimension instead of combining several, such as demographics, attitudes, and geography. Shoppers at Sam's Club, for example, represent a wide variety of incomes, education levels, and zip codes.

Consumer-Oriented Segmentation

Instead of falling into the traps, innovative segmenters step back from their products and look at consumer problems through consumers' eyes. They have insatiable curiosity and a willingness to ask a lot of questions, such as:

- How do consumers find out about products? How do they shop and compare alternatives?

- What are they looking for? What don't they have? What tradeoffs are they making? How do new benefits become important?

- What triggers a need? Which occasions? Which incentives?

- What steps do consumers take to satisfy their needs? When do consumers begin to think about a product, and when do they stop?

- Where do they look for solutions? Can they currently find them there?

Consider the consumer-oriented segmentation behind Gymboree's recent success in children's apparel. The company had discovered a segment of customers who were dissatisfied with the quality of children's clothing, as well as with the hectic experience of shopping with children.

Gymboree responded by launching an innovative specialty store offering well-made apparel and accessories for children under seven. The clothing is designed for style and wear, with roll-up cuffs for growing kids; durable, brightly colored fabrics; and exclusive designs that encourage mix-and-match pairings. The retail outlets are located in regional malls with high-end anchors. They have wide aisles for strollers and small children, and clothing is organized into wall groupings for easy shopping. Toys and videos are provided to keep children entertained, and the sales staff is compensated for attentive service, such as helping customers create multiple-item outfits.

Gymboree has done more than simply target the high-income shopper. It has singled out a segment of high-income shoppers who want distinctive, original clothing, *along with* a particular shopping experience. Gymboree doesn't just sell the right clothing—it sells an experience that leverages its founders' expertise in educational parent-child play groups.

Beyond the Here and Now

Innovative segmenters find growth by looking beyond current users. Most car-rental agencies, for example, focus on the business-travel market—locating their offices in airports and business districts. Enterprise Rent-a-Car, however, discovered an underserved segment in local residents who need a rental when their car is being repaired but find that traditional rental agencies are inconveniently located and charge more than their insurance will cover. To attract this insurance-compensated rental market, it introduced home pickup, lowered its prices, and established relationships with local claims adjusters. The move was so successful that Enterprise recently expanded to another underserved segment: people who need to rent an extra car for visiting guests. Knowing when and why people *don't* use a product can provide fertile ground for innovation and growth.

Toward a Richer Tool Kit

If all you want is to understand the world as it is today, traditional focus groups provide adequate information. To create a consumer-focused segmentation, however, you need a broader array of qualitative research tools that allow you to observe an activity as well as talk about it. Such tools include

- interviews conducted in consumers' homes, where they are observed using the product and its alternatives

- interviews conducted with consumers as they shop, to see how they compare products and get information

- wish lists in which consumers describe needs the product isn't satisfying

Thermos went beyond focus groups to observe firsthand how customers cooked on its electric grill in their own homes. What it discovered—that the grill was awkward for apartment dwellers to store and use—led the company to introduce a new oval design, with shelves and controls relocated for easier use on small balconies. Direct observation of people using the product in their own homes resulted in a design improvement that focus groups and survey research would have been less likely to discover.

Traditional market research, with its emphasis on collecting large amounts of statistically significant quantitative data, may be "scientific." Unfortunately, scientific validity all too often comes at the price of superficiality. At most companies, the people doing market research rarely have a deep understanding of the consumer. They are good at providing "data," but they can be prisoners of existing market definitions and research tools— whether those definitions and tools are relevant or not.

What's more, market research frequently amounts to little more than testing consumers' reactions to new ideas identified by the development organization. It's not designed to grasp their real experiences with products. The resulting information is nowhere near fine-grained enough to capture the imagination of senior managers, and it rarely serves as a catalyst for new ways to respond to real needs.

In addition to product-use observations, other kinds of tools can help innovators get a richer perspective on consumers' attitudes and lifestyles. They include

- anthropological studies that record a day in the life of the consumer, with an observer, a still camera, or a video camera

- *laddering*, which uses in-depth interviews that link products and benefits to deeply held values

- chat groups that promote continuing dialogue between consumers and innovators about the product, the activity, or life in general

The double vision of the true innovator comes from the ability to appreciate the richness of the consumer experience today and what it might be tomorrow. These visionaries are introducing new segmenting techniques into their standard marketing repertoire. The information they are acquiring is a competitive advantage that will be difficult to match.

This article was first published in August 1996.

David C. Edelman and Saba Malak

There is no more valuable—or more misunderstood—asset than customer information. In recent years, this has almost become an open secret  as companies attempt to gather information with as little knowledge of or involvement from their customers as possible. Yet by not engaging customers in the process of collecting and using information about themselves, marketers are missing a rare opportunity to build loyalty and advantage.

To be sure, most consumers are underwhelmed with current direct-marketing practices. In a recent survey of U.S. consumers, 50 percent said they would prefer not to get unsolicited mailings, 58 percent said they automatically discard them, and 78 percent said they favor laws prohibiting companies from using personal data for marketing. Yet 88 percent of the same consumers said they would gladly provide information to marketers in exchange for true value. The issue, clearly, is not one of privacy but of how information is collected and applied.

Is Anybody Home?

If marketers haven't responded, perhaps it's because they haven't been paying attention. We recently called the toll-free numbers of 50 randomly selected large companies. We explained that we used their products and asked to be put on a mailing list for more information. Only one-third of the companies had a database that could take names and addresses; only two companies inquired about family demographics; and just one asked where we bought the product and how we used it. Consumers want to communicate, but it seems as if most marketers haven't figured out how to listen.

That's beginning to change, however. Recently, a new breed of marketers has set out to harness the power in individual customer relationships. We call the strategy Segment-of-One marketing. These companies have built their entire businesses not around specific products or services but on the forthright use of customer information to unlock new avenues for delivering customized value. The group includes

- Individual Inc, a fax-delivered news service that provides articles on topics customers have selected

- Travelocity, an Internet service of American Airlines' SABRE and Travel Guides that makes airline reservations, keeps track of individual seating and meal preferences, and even notifies customers by e-mail when discount flights to preferred destinations are available

- 1-800-FLOWERS, a personal registry service that alerts customers to upcoming gift-giving occasions for family and friends and helps them choose a gift—flowers, candy, or even toys—on the basis of what they gave in the past

What's different about these companies is the way they interact with their customers. Rather than just push products, they stake their reputation on turning customer information into valued services. When they make a sale, it's on the customer's own terms, through a channel the customer chooses—a different model from junk mail and annoying dinnertime calls. Instead of creating problems, these marketers become problem solvers. It's a dynamic relationship in which both parties benefit as the customer discloses more and more information. The companies make selling a service instead of a nuisance.

Segment-of-One relationships not only entice customers to spend more (because the product or service is customized and the transaction quick and easy), they also encourage them to invest additional information to receive additional value. And the more they invest, the more costly and inconvenient it is for them to leave. When switching costs arise out of information that customers have invested in your company for future services, the bond can be compelling.

Firefly, a new service on the World Wide Web, is one company that is exploring the frontier of Segment-of-One marketing. It maintains constant communication with its "members" to learn what they like and don't like in music and movies. Then, by comparing its lists, it can suggest additional titles that other members with similar tastes have recommended. Customers will be able to sample these suggestions and place orders without ever having to enter a store.

Firefly also encourages participants to send in their own reviews to share with other members, and it even hosts chat forums for fans with similar interests. When the give-and-take of information goes this deep, customers are unlikely to start over with a new service. But they are likely to provide valuable word-of-mouth advertising when they talk with their friends about their on-line relationships.

A Brand Transformation

For traditional marketers with large-scale legacy systems, making the transition to a Segment-of-One strategy can be a considerable undertaking. In fact, all the start-ups cited above had the luxury of building their information databases and processes from scratch. But for many areas of the consumer goods industry, Segment-of-One databases are well worth considering. What's more, early movers will have the advantage because customers will be difficult to lure away once they've begun investing personal information in a service they like.

Becoming a Segment-of-One marketer has three important components: strategy, technology, and organization.

Strategy. Instead of thinking in terms of broad-scale reach, you must aim to maximize the value of each customer relationship. This perspective focuses you on the individual customer rather than on a particular product. 1-800-FLOWERS, for example, isn't in the business of selling flowers; it's in the business of serving its customers' gift-giving needs. Travelocity is neither SABRE nor American Airlines but a separate brand developed to provide a range of services, not just sell tickets.

Technology. Next, you need to select the right technology—especially if you have to migrate from legacy systems to a new environment. But remember: your database should be more than a passive source of lists to pull for a campaign. Rather, you should view it as an active partner that continuously sifts through information looking for patterns and triggers, provides access to other databases, and simplifies search and purchase transactions.

Organization. Perhaps most important, the Segment-of-One transformation will require reorienting the entire organization to a new way of thinking about the brand. Product and process management will continue to be key, but the overriding focus should be on communicating with customers during all product and service transactions.

Start Building Your Club

Before you launch your next direct-mail campaign—which at least 97 percent of your list is likely to ignore—consider how you can create a Segment-of-One relationship that can entice 100 percent into increased interaction with your brand.

Think of yourself as the founding member of a special club of consumers with common interests and needs that you can fulfill. To begin, ask yourself whom you want to invite, how you will find them, what you want to learn from them, how you'll communicate, and, above all, how you will keep them interested over time.

Today the most successful companies are the ones that customers know best. Tomorrow they'll be the ones that know their customers best.

This article was first published in February 1997.

Segment-of-One is a registered trademark of The Boston Consulting Group.

David Pecaut and Joan Dea

Most companies view their customers through a close-up lens. This limits their field of vision because they can see a consumer's reactions only to a specific product or service. Improvements may result from such proximity, but breakthroughs are rare. A few companies pull back to a midrange lens, which reveals dissatisfactions with a whole product or service category. This wider view opens up more opportunities.

As powerful as a complete view of a category can be, however, companies often achieve the most innovative breakthroughs by stepping back even further to a wide-angle lens. This permits a holistic view of the dissatisfactions that permeate consumers' lives (see Exhibit 11). We call these broad-based dissatisfactions *consumer distempers*.

Exhibit 11

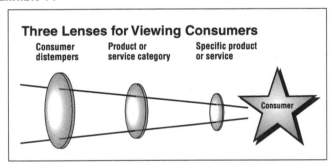

Three Lenses for Viewing Consumers

Consumer distempers | Product or service category | Specific product or service

Consumer

An understanding of these distempers reveals growth opportunities that the other lenses miss. But the wide-angle lens is rarely used; in fact, most companies are stuck in close-up mode.

How President's Choice Achieved Breakthroughs

President's Choice, a private-label premium food brand sold in Canada's Loblaw's stores, has successfully looked at the grocery consumer through all three lenses. By using midrange and wide-angle lenses, President's Choice has established levels of quality and customer loyalty unusual in the grocery business. In fact, President's Choice has single-handedly repositioned Loblaw's from being an also-ran in Canadian food retailing to being a clear leader.

After looking at its products through the traditional close-up lens, President's Choice decided to deliver better quality than the leading brands but at the same price. For example, its popular Decadent Chocolate Chip Cookies are made with butter and contain more chips than most leading brands.

Next, by using a midrange lens, President's Choice redefined the food category by broadening it. Shoppers customarily look for individual foods, using their own inventiveness to combine them into meals. President's Choice saw the need for prepared meals and sauces, and for ready-to-eat foods such as prepeeled shrimp, to make meal preparation easier and quicker. By offering those items and encouraging customers through its marketing and in-store merchandising, President's Choice also builds experimentation into the shopping experience.

Finally, President's Choice used a wide lens to discover consumer distempers. It saw that people crave a sense of community. Traditional ties—with local shopkeepers or neighbors—used to provide such a connection. Today, for many reasons, including television, long commutes, and the impersonality of shopping malls, many people feel disconnected from their communities. Indeed, consumer research shows that, as busy and as focused on themselves as people are, they yearn to fill the void left by the weakening of traditional ties.

President's Choice has fostered a sense of affiliation through its "Insiders' Report." Begun in 1983 and distributed with the daily newspaper, this guide advertises specials and also contains food tips, recipes, and stories about how President's Choice developed its new products. By 1993, it was the most widely circulated publication in Canada, reaching more people than the *Toronto Star*, the daily with the largest circulation in the country. By combining consumer participation with an aura of exclusivity, President's Choice has built a loyal following.

President's Choice has also recognized that many consumers feel pressed for time or money, and that many have an innate skepticism about business—a feeling of *us* against *them*. By addressing the distempers that arise from shortages of time and money, as well as the desire for affiliation, President's Choice has earned consumers' trust. It saves people time because they don't need to shop around. It saves them money because its products exceed traditional private labels in quality but not price. Many of the offerings are kitchen time-savers and taste better than most meals prepared at home.

Today, President's Choice is the largest single brand in Loblaw's stores. The brand has been earning a net profit margin three or four times the industry norm of 1.5 to 2 percent for national brands. President's Choice can attribute its success to a coordinated three-lens perspective.

The Four Distempers

Companies ready to move beyond traditional product-satisfaction research need to focus on consumer distempers that yield the greatest breakthrough potential. The Boston Consulting Group's own wide-lens research has identified four distempers that hold huge potential for many companies: time pressure, financial insecurity, skepticism about business, and lack of affiliation.

Time Pressure. Those most affected by time pressure are working people between the ages of 25 and 55, particularly women. Working women with families typically have about one hour of personal time a day—one hour to get dressed, take a shower, read, and socialize. But these breadwinners would like to have more time—for example, to be with their families. Products such as prepared meals allow them to spend more time at the dinner table and less in the kitchen.

When U.S. consumers were asked in 1997 to define a fast meal, their most common answer was "five minutes." In 1992 it was 30 minutes. There have been dramatic increases in convenience store shopping, despite higher prices. In fact, the fastest-growing segment of the major oil companies in the U.S. today is retail operations collocated with gas stations. They address multiple needs at one site: gas, an instant meal, a beverage, and a snack. In casual clothing, the Gap has excelled at providing a full line of high-quality apparel at competitive prices. It offers one-stop shopping for items ranging from socks and underwear to pants, shirts, and dresses for the casually hip. In a wide variety of categories, helping the consumer deal with time pressure has become almost the defining element of many breakthrough strategies.

Financial Insecurity. Most people feel financially insecure—and with good reason. Over the past 20 years, the 60 percent of U.S. households with the lowest income have seen their net earnings decline by 5 to 15 percent. But even though the highest-paid one-fifth of households earn half of the total available income, the other four-fifths still offer tremendous potential. They control billions of purchasing dollars, yet few companies have tried to target them by addressing their financial insecurity. Coffee specialist Starbucks is one that did: it recognized the intense need for "affordable luxuries" in financially stretched Middle America. Used-car retailer CarMax is another: it saw a market among people who could only afford a used car but still deserved a superior shopping experience. By guaranteeing product quality, fair pricing, and a broad, convenient selection, CarMax seized a break-through opportunity.

Skepticism About Business. Consumers are unwilling to believe standard brand claims and often think that advertising emphasizes irrelevant and confusing differences. Companies pour countless dollars into television commercials that consumers often zap with an expertly handled remote. When they do see the ads, their typical response is, "At best it's enter-tainment; at worst it's a waste of time." Companies are losing the ability to connect with their customers. Yet when consumers find a brand they believe they can trust, they often move beyond loyalty to become brand apostles.

Lack of Affiliation. So far, only a few companies have developed brands that try to build community by encouraging consumer involvement, but the potential appeal of this approach is enormous. Starbucks, for example, rec-ognized the power of coffee bars to foster a sense of community. Its mission is to be the "third place" for its customers after home and work.

Lack of affiliation may be the most powerful distemper because it opens up the possibility of an entirely different type of brand strategy. Most com-panies manage their brand image by communicating with consumers as indi-viduals, whereas companies promoting affiliation see the relationship of consumers with one another as equally profound. These new affiliation-oriented brands gain power by creating a communal experience that transcends the benefits provided by their products alone. As they do so, their value propositions become deeply embedded in the emotional lives of their customers.

Using Your Advantages to Address Consumer Distempers

Traditional close-up-lens techniques—such as product- or purchase-satisfac-tion surveys, conjoint analysis, statistical market research, and tracking studies—are often the enemy of breakthrough insight. Wide-lens analysis digs deeper into the emotional undercurrents of people's lives, where the biggest opportunity to create a lasting bond between the individual and the brand lies. Today's brand manager must connect seamlessly with consumers, observe their behavior closely, and understand in a way that is raw and real how they use products and services. That knowledge will help the brand man-ager address traditional category needs as well as distempers.

There are strong traditional advantages in many businesses: an established consumer base, proven products, long-standing channel relationships, and, most important, the power of a recognized brand name. Not many companies have the vision and persistence to use those advantages to address consumer distempers. That failure creates a tremendous potential payoff for the companies that do.

This article was first published in April 1998.

CUSTOMER RETENTION: BEYOND BRIBES AND GOLDEN HANDCUFFS

Thierry Chassaing, David C. Edelman, and Lynn Segal

The battleground isn't market share anymore. It's share of time, share of stomach, share of wallet. Competitors are coming from out of nowhere  to steal away your best customers. Takeout stores are taking on packaged foods. Sneaker companies are slipping into clothing. Long-established companies are on the defensive and scrambling to take the offensive. They're looking for quick and easy ways to bring in new customers and lock in old ones. Some of the most popular shortcuts, however, are turning into complicated and expensive detours.

The Seduction of Information Nirvana

Many companies have been counting on their customer databases to be the silver bullet in their customer-retention arsenal. With timely information flowing through electronic channels, they expect to be able to anticipate their customers' behavior and, in some cases, to control it.

However, one manifestation of the new technology—the customer loyalty program—is turning out to add as much as 8 percent to the cost of each sale. Moreover, while customers are happy enough to be rewarded for buying, bonuses rarely raise their opinion of inherently weak brands. To be sure, a well-designed loyalty program coupled with a strong brand can increase both share and demand; but no loyalty program, no matter how well designed, can rehabilitate an inferior brand or make up for poor service.

Another technology that was supposed to help attract and retain customers—the information superhighway—has failed so far to provide a lasting advantage to any players. Most marketers envisioned the electronic channel as a one-way street that they would control. In fact, it has become a crowded freeway, open to consumers and competitors alike. Through the Internet, consumers and their search agents are increasingly able to compare prices, rate products, and locate the best value. Meanwhile, competitors are buying high-value-consumer lists on the open market. The result is that a small group of the most desirable targets get bombarded with incentives—really, bribes—for switching everything from credit cards to long-distance phone service. The technology that was expected to enable marketers to attract and retain customers is undermining that very goal.

Attracting the Right Customers

Customer retention may be more complicated than most marketers realized, but that doesn't mean the goal should be abandoned. Loyal customers *do* generate more value, especially when you consider the marginal costs of attracting masses of new customers, many of whom don't return. Industry after industry has seen significantly higher returns from loyal customers than from occasional ones. Frequent diners in midprice restaurants, for instance, offer 10 times the return of "special night out" visitors. And cosmetics customers loyal to one brand are worth more than 15 times the value of infrequent purchasers.

The objective, however, isn't necessarily to try to retain all customers; it's to retain the best ones. If you build an economic model of behavior and segment customers on the basis of frequency of purchase, average margin, and loyalty, you'll probably find that many customers just aren't worth keeping. For some companies, a 20 percent attrition rate may be appropriate, especially if the right 80 percent are staying.

How do you retain the best customers? As simple as it sounds, you have to earn their loyalty the old-fashioned way: with products that reflect a deep understanding of their needs, tiered service levels that pamper them, and sufficient insight to anticipate their future needs. There are no silver bullets.

What Do Your Best Customers Want?

To increase your share of your best customers' purchases, the first step is to discover why they've been your best customers so far. Chances are you'll find a combination of three reasons: they believe you offer the best value; they believe your company's products or services are reliable; and they know that you sometimes reward them for staying or penalize them for switching. This dynamic can be expressed as a simple equation:

Retention = Superior Value + Trust + High Switching Cost

The problem with most retention programs is that they focus unduly on switching costs—bribes and golden handcuffs—which, for your best customers, are the least compelling of the three factors. The customers who buy your most profitable products have been doing so primarily because they appreciate those products and trust your company. To encourage them to buy more, you need to focus on broadening and deepening your product line. That involves looking beyond the product to how your customers experience it.

This is precisely what *Sports Illustrated* did when it set out to learn why its most loyal readers subscribed. To its surprise, it discovered not one but four different experiences of its product. For the first group, the magazine was pure escape; for the second, it provided a source of sports trivia; for the third, it was a collectible; and for the fourth, it served as a how-to guide. Same product, different experiences. Once *Sports Illustrated* understood this, it could enrich those experiences with specialized lines of books, videos, and CD/ROMs, a kids' magazine, and travel packages to sporting events.

Test, Learn, and Revise

Focusing on value and trust is neither quick nor easy. It certainly is harder than trying to manipulate customers with carrots and sticks. Some customers value everyday low prices; others, continuous innovation. Either way, you need to insert the qualities each group values into every point of contact. That means thinking about those connection points differently. Your internal operations may be organized around marketing, sales, and after-sales service; but to customers, their experience is a single one with your brand's name all over it—from hearing about the product, to shopping for it, to buying it, to getting it delivered, to getting it repaired.

You have to know when you've achieved the right balance in the retention equation. That's why it's crucial to test, learn, and revise as you go. Keeping ahead of your best customers requires constant adjustment. Sometimes you'll have the "right" experience but for the wrong customer, or vice versa. Once you know that you have the right formula, you can align your processes and people to embed it in all aspects of your customers' experience with your brand. If you do it well, your loyal customers will become your loyal advocates. You can't have too much of that kind of advertising.

To focus on what your customers really value:

- Don't assume that all customers experience your product the same way. Concentrate on enhancing the qualities your best customers value, and recognize that there may be more than one way to experience your product.

- Don't think in narrow, functional boxes. Discover how your best customers experience your brand from the time they learn about it through purchase, use, service, and disposal.

- Don't worry about all defectors. Not all customers are worth keeping. Force your competitors to serve the ones you don't want.

Customer retention is a moving target because what people want is constantly changing. The product that delights them one year might bore them the next. Moreover, your competitors are always catching up by imitating you, and technology is always introducing new features. Nevertheless, your customers are your assets. Cultivate them or lose them. To understand the richness of your customer base, develop different messages for different audiences, create tiered levels of service, and lock in your best customers with the best you can offer. Then you can deliver superior value and trustworthiness, which, over the long term, are more likely than bribes and handcuffs to retain your most profitable customers.

This article was first published in May 1998.

ONE SIZE DOESN'T FIT ALL

Jeannine Bergers Everett and Barbara B. Hulit

In an ideal world, producers and retailers would know what individual consumers like and dislike, as well as how much they purchase and how often. In the real world, marketers rely on statistical averages—32 percent of consumers "agree" and 68 percent "disagree." But it's easy to forget that such averages are only abstractions, calculated by generalizing about groups of people with different backgrounds, tastes, and opinions. Just as aggregated price and cost data can conceal both opportunities and losses within a product portfolio, so can market research averages obscure profitable segments. Marketers who haven't looked closely at consumers may be missing opportunities to design products and services that they really like, as well as to fix the ones they don't.

Why are statistical averages no longer adequate to describe the market? For one thing, the mass market is losing its homogeneity as consumers seek to distinguish themselves through their purchases. For another, consumers not only look for distinctive products, they also look for better ones. With limited time and patience for shopping, consumers want the right product right now.

Most companies have long known about the benefits of segmentation and targeted marketing. Nevertheless, when it comes to meeting the needs of their markets, they tend to drift toward the middle. For example, there are many people who enjoy spicy food, but there are many more who don't. So the former have to settle for "piquant" when they really want "five alarm." Both segments are compromised, and no one is happy.

Why, then, are so many products positioned in a vanilla land that doesn't excite anyone? The answer is that, despite their efforts to segment the market, most companies still develop merchandising strategies from a mass-market perspective. If you want to do more than satisfy consumers, you have to bend a few rules and adopt some fresh approaches.

You Don't Have to Be All Things to All People

The size of the mainstream market is seductive. It's easy to give in to the temptation to water down a potentially polarizing product, making it less idiosyncratic. But attempts at moderation can drive away the most loyal customers, and the resulting product may still be too far from the center to appeal to the masses.

This failing is common among food companies that target preschoolers. Children go through rapid developmental changes during their first five years. Between their first and second years, for example, they require foods that are easy to swallow and to handle themselves. Toddlers respond well to bland flavors, small portions, and easy-to-pick-up pieces. As they approach their fourth year, children want to take control, so they like foods with do-it-yourself features, such as sprinkles and mix-ins. Their desire for fun is greater than their need for assistance. Many companies, however, develop broad product lines, hoping to appeal to children of all ages. These foods are too mushy and dull-tasting for older children but too hard for younger ones to eat. The products miss both targets.

You Don't Have to Define the Category—Let the Consumer Do It

Lifestyle brands—brands that are integral to a targeted segment's way of life—tend to cross product categories. Therefore, to create a lifestyle brand, a company needs to do more than identify functional preferences for a particular product. It must develop a thorough understanding of its targeted consumers' broader aspirations. What are they trying to achieve through particular purchases?

Understanding this concept has allowed such specialty retailers as Frontgate to sell $3,000 grills in addition to pools and camping equipment. It has helped the Gap expand into personal-care products, and Crate & Barrel extend its reach beyond kitchenware into home furnishings. A lifestyle brand is an umbrella for products that create and enhance a way of life, not just one activity.

You Don't Have to Be the Biggest Brand in the Category

It's time to rethink the concept of size. A successful brand should be the first choice of its target group, but that group doesn't have to encompass everyone. Large profits and brisk inventory turnover can result from many people buying a product occasionally, a few people buying it frequently, or a few people paying a premium for an added feature they can't get anywhere else.

One example is frozen pizza. Most people love pizza, and the overall category experienced double-digit growth for more than a decade. Yet during the same period, the frozen pizza category declined. Although the product was inexpensive, consumers were dissatisfied with its flavor, texture, and skimpy toppings. Kraft's response: DiGiorno Rising Crust Pizza—a better-tasting, self-rising frozen pizza with higher-quality ingredients, selling at an unheard-of price of more than $6. Clearly, not everyone was looking for restaurant-quality frozen pizza at a premium price. But by understanding the needs and dissatisfactions of its target market, Kraft created a winner. Today DiGiorno pizza boasts retail sales of more than $200 million and is Kraft's most successful new-product introduction.

By serving a specialty market particularly well, a company can also attract consumers from the mainstream. Like DiGiorno, Starbucks Coffee started out targeting a narrow segment. It focused on U.S. coffee drinkers who, perhaps having traveled in Europe, wanted a neighborhood café where they could sit and drink European-style coffees. But the company ended up converting so many mainstream consumers that it has been able to extend its brand to ice creams, ceramics, CDs, and other products.

You Don't Always Have to Advertise

Advertising is expensive. So is using samples and coupons. And communicating in the mass media isn't precise enough to reach closely targeted consumer markets. Targeted consumers require targeted marketing methods. The goal is to create "apostles" for your brand. Apostles are those customers who are so pleased with your product that they take over the advertising themselves. They tell family members and friends, who tell their relatives and friends, and so on. Commercial advertising has yet to come up with a tool that beats word-of-mouth advocacy.

But how do you turn your customers into apostles? In targeted marketing, *where* you communicate is as important as *what* you communicate. Where do your targeted consumers live and work? What hobbies and activities fill their days? What do they read?

You can reach mothers of small children, for example, through pediatricians and play programs such as those organized by Gymboree, or on Web sites targeted to parents. Young urbanites hang out in coffee bars, tote city magazines, and go to restaurants, theaters, and fitness centers. You can use pattern-matching algorithms to group grocery shoppers on the basis of the contents of their shopping carts—oil, eggs, milk, and baby food, for example, or refrigerated pasta, salad dressing, and coffee beans. Cross-marketing or stores-within-stores are new ways to reach consumers. You don't have to incur the costs of traditional advertising to reap its benefits.

If you suspect that you haven't done all you can to win lifetime loyalty from the full range of your market, consider the following questions:

- Do you compete in a market dominated by only a few undifferentiated players? This was the case a decade ago for many brands, especially in the cosmetics industry. Eventually, products made for individual skin types and preferences usurped market share from their complacent competitors.

- Can you describe your customers with as much detail as you can describe your favorite film or television characters? Beyond age and sex, do you know who your customers are and who they want to be? What they have and what they lack? How they live and where they play?

- Have you ever dismissed an idea as unrealistic only to have a smaller company pick it up, run with it, and win? Have you examined your product pipeline for the small ideas that could grow into big ones?

- Do you continually search for the big idea that will overtake the whole market, yet never find it? Maybe that "big idea" is really a series of small initiatives.

- Do you offer a lot of "different" product flavors that use the same formulas and recipes? This may be a sign that although your goal was to offer real choice, the differences became watered down.

One size doesn't fit all. Consumers buy shoes to fit *their* feet, not average feet. Market research often comes up with an average answer, but average answers satisfy no one completely. By reaching for "lovers," not simply users, marketers create apostles—people who buy more, pay more, and spread the word.

This article was first published in January 1999.

Part Five

THE BRAND

David C. Edelman and Michael J. Silverstein

A business revolution has come to brands. From every side, traditional brands appear to be under attack. Costs are escalating. Consumer loyalty is eroding.

Retailers are competing through private-label products. Store brands are commandeering valuable niches. Some observers are even speculating about "the end of brands."

No, brands won't disappear. But what a brand is and how best to manage it are changing. Increasingly, a brand is far more than just a name on a product. Winning brands are carefully designed business systems. These systems stretch from the choice of raw materials to final service with the customer. And it is the total system that the customer purchases, not just the product.

When brands become business systems, brand management becomes far too important to leave to the marketing department. It cuts across functions and business processes. It requires decisions and actions at every point along the value chain. It is central to a company's overall business strategy. That's why we call it total brand management.

Escalating Investments, Increased Focus

Total brand management can take a variety of forms:

- In some cases, the brand extends beyond the actual product to include the infrastructure supporting it. For example, high-end brands such as Lexus or Infiniti, and even midmarket brands such as General Electric appliances, have invested heavily in information systems that support customer service and serve as marketing attributes enhancing the core product.

- In other cases, well-crafted umbrella brands like Gillette or Levi's stretch across many related products, enabling their owners to leverage materials innovations, marketing investments, and trade promotions more effectively.

- In still other cases, the entire retail system itself is the brand. At The Body Shop, for example, the way products are sourced (all-natural ingredients), developed (no animal testing), and sold (in distinctive Body Shop boutiques) is as important to the company's marketing image as the products themselves.

Regardless of the particular form, total brand management has two fundamental imperatives. The first is a major escalation in the amount and kind of investments necessary to support a successful brand. It's no longer enough simply to increase the advertising budget. Companies have to invest in a broad range of costly capabilities: proprietary research methodologies for understanding subtle shifts in consumer attitudes, intertwined manufacturing and logistics networks providing superior retail service at lower cost, retail information-processing capability to optimize inventory costs, and product development functions to speed product innovation.

But the total brand manager must also remember that such investments are only table stakes that allow entry into the game. It takes more than deep pockets to win. In particular, companies must concentrate on three key high-leverage activities:

Maximize Synergies Across a Coherent Brand Portfolio. Financing a massive buildup in new capabilities requires spreading investments over many brands, cascading across price points and channels. Practitioners of total brand management, therefore, focus not on individual brands but on a *coherent brand portfolio.*

French cosmetics maker L'Oréal, for example, knew that increased R&D was essential to competing in the new brand environment. So over a five-year period, L'Oréal doubled its R&D budget. This major investment helped spark a key innovation: the company's new "anti-aging complex"— a breakthrough in skin care that slows the onset and spread of wrinkles. But L'Oréal was able to afford this massive increase in R&D spending only because it could spread the costs over several brands in its portfolio at different price points and positions. The company introduced its anti-aging complex under the Lancôme brand, then moved it into the Vichy range and finally into broad distribution with Plénitude. It has been a tremendously successful innovation, but it couldn't have been accomplished with one brand alone.

The key word in "coherent brand portfolio" is *coherent.* It does no good to cobble together a collection of unrelated brands. Doing so leads only to higher overhead costs, fragmented business processes, and duplication of resources.

Not all brands contribute equally to enhancing the value of a company's brand portfolio. Brand managers must evaluate each existing brand along two dimensions: its fit with core capability and its potential for value generation. Such an assessment reshuffles the brands into four categories of investment priority, ranging from good fit/high value to low fit/low value.

Strengthen the Brand Portfolio Through Innovation. As the L'Oréal example suggests, innovation is more important now than ever. Other forms of growth, such as acquisitions and expanding margins, have been largely played out. Spending on retailers or consumers is becoming too expensive for all but the biggest budgets. What's more, consumers are becoming more sophisticated and harder to reach. Mere bells and whistles won't sell anymore.

But the kind of innovation that matters is not what managers might expect. It's not the creation of new brands—an increasingly expensive proposition. Rather, it is the reinvention of existing brands through three basic techniques: repositioning, extension, and transformation.

For example, SmithKline Beecham repositioned Lucozade, once considered a medicinal remedy, by directing it at anybody who cares about health, particularly athletes. Today, Lucozade is Britain's number one non-cola drink. Unilever extended Flora, originally a "healthy fat" margarine low in polyunsaturates, across product categories to become an umbrella brand for a whole range of health-food oils and dairy products. And by moving quickly to exploit a technological breakthrough, Procter & Gamble transformed its traditional Pert Shampoo brand by launching a two-in-one shampoo/conditioner known as PertPlus.

Secure the Brand Through Close Relationships with Customers and the Trade. Increasingly, customers value the reassurance and stability that come from an enduring relationship with someone who understands and can respond to their specific needs. But this requires a broad rethinking of the value a company offers its customers, as well as of the specific products and services it provides.

Not long ago, for example, Japanese video-game maker Nintendo found itself in a dying market with too many players and limited shelf space. The challenge: to discover a new way to hold its brand name with customers. So the company launched two new business initiatives: *Nintendo Power,* a $15-a-year magazine that receives 40,000 letters a month, and a 900 number on game strategy that receives 10,000 calls a week. Both proved to be powerful customer-relationship vehicles that cut across hardware, software, education, new product development, and customer service. But even more important, the magazine and the 900 number have opened a direct line of communication from the customer back to new product development, which has enabled the company to forecast sales of a new product within 10 percent. Today, with annual sales of $5 billion, Nintendo is Japan's most profitable company.

For many brands, the most important customer is the trade. To fend off private-label growth, brand managers must find ways to create value for the trade without simply giving away more margin. A leading office-products manufacturer, for example, has been able to work with a superstore chain to develop new packaging, replenishment, and stocking systems that provide more margin to the chain than private-label products would. With its interlocking business systems, the manufacturer can now secure its brand franchise and increase margins in a win-win relationship with a heavily deal-driven retailer.

The Role of the Total Brand Manager: Making Choices Along the Entire Value Chain

As brand managers manage portfolios of brands, customer segments, and retailers across an entire business system, their role has become more cross-functional and strategic. Indeed, total brand management often involves redesigning the business through new partnerships, better cross-functional linkages, and innovation. To that end, brand managers must make choices at every point along the value chain, not just in marketing and sales.

This more strategic conception of brands means that the stakes involved in launching, maintaining, and evolving a brand are higher. But so are the potential payoffs. Companies that innovate new brand-building strategies will reap long-term rewards. Those that do not will slowly disappear.

This article was first published in 1993.

David Pecaut

Many brands today are dying. Not the natural death of obsolescence but a slow, painful death of sales and margin erosion. The managers of these  brands are not complacent. In fact, they are constantly tweaking the advertising, pricing, and cost of their products. At the heart of the problem is a more fundamental issue: Can the original promise of the brand be re-created and a new spark lit with today's consumers? We believe it can. Most brands can be reinvented through a brand renaissance.

Parallels with the Past

The Renaissance of the fifteenth and sixteenth centuries reinvented the Greco-Roman artistic tradition. In the Dark Ages that followed the Greek and Roman eras, the church had declared realistic art too sensual and pagan. Rigid new standards were adopted and followed so thoroughly that the rules and techniques used to create the masterpieces of Greco-Roman art were forgotten. The artistic principles of antiquity had to be rediscovered at the start of the Renaissance.

Today, many companies have forgotten what made their brands great— they are lost in their own Dark Ages. Ineffective business practices have become habit, and the powerful connection of great brands to their customers has stagnated or died. Following in the footsteps of Renaissance artists, business managers can learn from the great art of antiquity.

The Essence of Great Art

Five elements of the Greco-Roman artistic tradition were rediscovered during the Renaissance. When applied to business practice, they can create a brand renaissance today.

1. **Sound economics.** Great art can flourish only under a system of competitive advantage that creates wealth. In the Renaissance, the city-states of Florence and Venice created economies with clear trading and banking advantages that generated great wealth. That wealth funded Renaissance art. Similarly, great brands can thrive only when a company's underlying economic system is sound.

2. **Profound insight.** Great art requires profound, often intuitive insight into human nature and values. Enduring brands are built on deep insights into consumers' needs and, especially, dissatisfactions. Consider, for example, the insights into unmet consumer needs represented by two recent brand successes. Starbucks Coffee has positioned itself as an affordable luxury for U.S. coffee lovers, and Saturn has provided a refreshing answer for many Americans yearning for a high-quality small car made in the U.S. and sold in an honest, "main street" kind of way.

3. **An original paradigm.** Great artists often invent their own rules. Seminal figures of Renaissance sculpture like Donatello and Ghiberti drew heavily on Greco-Roman models but developed original styles that influenced a host of imitators. Companies wishing to resuscitate moribund brands often look to classic models like Coke and Crest for inspiration, but most of the time a successful brand renaissance requires an original paradigm.

4. **Skilled teams.** The great art of antiquity and the Renaissance was often created by skilled teams working toward a common vision, under the direction of a master. Chief sculptor Phidias, for example, designed and supervised all the figures of the Parthenon, but no one knows which, if any, were actually created by him. The teams that rebuild great brands may be led by visionaries, but their success is founded equally on their members' collective and complementary skills.

5. **Relentless innovation.** Great art has always been driven by a stubborn pursuit of innovation. True artists don't create great works and then say, "Aha, that's it! I'll just repeat that over and over." They push the boundaries. Sustaining strong brands takes the same dedication to innovation and improvement in all aspects of brand management: positioning, product development, marketing, and the coordination of the entire consumer experience.

Achieving a Brand Renaissance

Is this arts-to-brands analogy a useful way to think about business and brands? We think so. Consider the example of Nike.

In 1984, Nike's profits plummeted because the running craze had ended and the company didn't have a new product to replace its running shoes.

Nike's managers weren't strong marketers; they were running enthusiasts. But company founder Phil Knight went back to the drawing board and reinvented Nike around customer segmentation and brand management. The company's shareholder return grew spectacularly as Nike trounced its original sports-shoe competitor, Adidas, and, more recently, Reebok.

Nike achieves deep insight into consumers, but not through conventional research. Every Nike shoe designer has to spend several weeks on the road each year, living with target customers—hanging out at playgrounds and tennis courts, going to sports clubs—and watching how they behave. Then Nike uses its large investment in technology to develop innovative shoes that respond to the physical and emotional needs of its customers.

Nike's most powerful marketing idea has been to redefine how to think about shoe categories. The company has continually subsegmented and expanded categories. In 1985 a basketball shoe was a basketball shoe. Nike segmented basketball-shoe customers according to their physical needs and personal aspirations. For example, the technology in the Air Jordan is aimed at shooting guards, who land with about three times their body weight and for whom quickness and shooting prowess are paramount. The Air Force, which Charles Barkley wears, is designed for a different body weight, different structural needs, and a different attitude toward life and sport.

Nike also uses design and color to subsegment and expand categories. The original Air Jordan was a bright red, causing the NBA to ban the shoe initially. A woman once criticized a Matisse painting by saying, "I never saw a woman look like that!" Matisse is said to have responded, "Madam, that is not a woman. It is a painting." Nike might have said, "That is not a basketball shoe. It is an Air Jordan."

All five elements of brand renaissance are evident in Nike's resurgence.

- Nike built a powerful economic system founded on low-cost outsourced manufacturing in the Far East and sophisticated channel management. This system helps generate the financial returns to support brand building.

- Nike develops deep insights about its target customers, which, taken together with its ability to subsegment markets, allow it to connect with the aspirations of many different people, from playground basketball fanatics to middle-aged occasional joggers.

- Nike also created an original brand paradigm. While remaining true to the brand's foundation on superior athletic performance, Nike added a focus on sport as style and, when it eventually succeeded in the aerobics category, on sport as self-realization. "Just Do It," Nike's slogan, has proved a powerful and unique emotional touchstone for sports enthusiasts around the globe.

- Nike's culture resembles a Renaissance studio in its ability to remain focused on its inspirational raison d'être while executing the mundane details of brand management day in and day out. This spirit is sustained in the cross-functional design, marketing, and management teams at headquarters, as well as in one of the most effective sales and technical support organizations serving retail America.

- Nike has relentlessly pursued improvement. Even as it succeeds, the organization is constantly pushing the limits of the brand's franchise by entering new categories and countries and innovating in all aspects of brand management.

Re-creating the Inspiration

Aspiring to a brand renaissance demands a complex and insightful perspective on the customer's experience and on the entire business system that defines a brand. The investment can be substantial, as can the required managerial expertise. But if the stakes are high, so are the potential payoffs. In a world where products, markets, channels, and industry boundaries are changing continually, a well-managed brand can be the foundation of future business profitability and the source of growth through new markets, new product segments, and even entire new businesses.

This article was first published in May 1996.

THE BRANDNET COMPANY

Antonella Mei-Pochtler and Philip Airey

A new kind of company—we call it the brandnet—is revolutionizing traditional marketing. Brands like Virgin, Swatch, Disney, Samuel Adams, Nike, and Adidas have become powerful images in consumers' minds, with a significance that transcends their association with any single product or service. Brandnet companies achieve more with less by

- accessing scale economies with limited volumes
- acquiring expertise without hiring it
- borrowing technology without developing it
- delivering to rapidly growing demand without creating redundant capacity
- growing with limited resources and investment

In brief, brandnet companies add value to their brand by transforming a conventional value chain into a value-adding network.

Brandnet companies look and feel different. Instead of inflexible investments, they have contractors and partners. They trade license fees, selectively contract production and distribution, broker sales forces, and share R&D. As a result, they gain access to best practices in every step of the value network and earn extraordinary returns with fewer assets.

Brandnet companies, however, maintain *complete control* over those activities that are critical to the customer's experience of the brand, and they perform them extremely well. More important, brandnet companies understand how to extend the brand's core value over multiple businesses, products, customers, and price points. They do this by establishing a strong emotional connection with consumers. And they can do it quickly.

Brandnet companies don't believe in borders—not for their products or their businesses. Producers such as Disney and Nike, for example, have opened their own retail outlets, while brandnet retailers, such as Benetton, are getting involved in managing their suppliers' value chains. Isn't this risky? Doesn't it invite brand dilution? Not necessarily. As long as the new idea is consistent with the brand's emotional appeal, it actually enhances the brand's relevance and vibrancy.

Zeroing In on the Customer's Experience

Brandnet companies distinguish themselves not by what they own (which could be very little) but by how they act. Their advantage is their ability to direct the core processes and players that ensure a superior experience of the brand. Therefore, determining which processes and capabilities to focus on is as important as which businesses, markets, and product lines to pursue. Core processes might include production and design, positioning, targeting, standards, guarantees, retail displays, and unique combinations of benefits.

Should you be concerned about brandnet organizations? You bet! With their intense focus on brand value and their low asset base, brandnet companies are extremely agile. Eschewing heavy investments in facilities and resources, they can move quickly in several directions at once. That means they can come at you from out of nowhere and steal share away overnight.

The Virgin Phenomenon

Virgin is the classic brandnet company. Founded in 1970 by Richard Branson as a discount-record and mail-order operation, the British company has extended its brand to airlines, financial services, retail stores, railroads, and hotels. With a total turnover approaching £1.5 billion, Virgin comprises more than 250 companies, joint ventures, and partnerships in a variety of businesses from personal computers to soft drinks.

Virgin is more than a collection of disparate products under a provocative name, however. Whether it's a music video or an airline flight, customers experience the Virgin brand as something new, exciting, and different. How did this come about? When Branson started his first business, he understood that he wasn't only fulfilling a need for discount music. He was also affirming his customers' *taste* in music, as well as giving them a sense of *affinity* with a group of like-minded alternative-music fans. He made his customers feel *special*, and that emotional connection generated a passionate loyalty to, and trust in, the brand.

A more significant accomplishment has been Branson's ability to extend this emotional response to other products and services—most notably, airline travel. Filling a void left by Freddie Laker in low-cost international flights, Branson offered first-class service at business-class prices. Where was the connection with his other businesses? It was in the brand experience. Branson put the romance back into flying. He made his customers feel special with such services as massages, limousine transportation, and seat-back videos. Established competitors on Virgin routes were unwilling to enter the escalated amenity war.

Branson focuses on lean operations and contracts out or leases much of his operations. But Virgin staffs all the elements of the business system that are critical to the customer's emotional connection with the brand—on the ground and in the air—including reservations, ground check-in, marketing, sales, and in-flight services.

Branson delivers on this experience over and over again, in business after business. Customers have learned to trust him, to know that he won't let them down. Not surprisingly, Virgin has a 93 percent brand recognition in the U.K. In fact, when a BBC poll recently asked 1,200 people who should be charged with rewriting the Ten Commandments, Branson scored fourth—after Mother Teresa, the pope, and the Archbishop of Canterbury.

Competing Against a Brandnet Player

Adidas reacted to Nike's highly networked business model by radically restructuring its value chain around the core functions of R&D, design, and the retail experience. By shedding its production facilities, it achieved the flexibility it needed to surf the new trends in the fickle sports-shoe world. A lean and aggressive brand-focused management made this possible, and the company benefited significantly. In the past three years, Adidas's sales have grown by more than 70 percent, and operating earnings continue to climb in 1997.

Companies with weaker brands might opt for another route. They could become a strategic pillar within another company's brand network—a copacker or service provider, for example. Private-label producers like Drypers in diapers, Hochland in processed cheese, or S. Benedetto in soft drinks have successfully chosen this direction.

Which route you take depends on your starting point and capabilities. Strong global branders with superior technology and innovation, such as Gillette or Procter & Gamble, will manage these functions on a globally integrated basis. Even the strongest players, however, might benefit from the asset stripping pioneered by the brandnet companies. Regional competence branders like Beiersdorf's Nivea or Barilla's Mulino Bianco might opt for stronger outsourcing or share key functions with other regional players to compensate for scale disadvantages. This doesn't mean that they don't control these functions—they just don't own them exclusively.

Is There a Brandnet in Your Future?

To determine how well you would fare against the sudden appearance of a stealth brandnetter or to decide whether to become one yourself, ask yourself the following questions:

1. Does my brand resonate with customers on a powerful emotional level? Have I exploited this across all possible categories?

2. What functions in the value chain contribute most to my customers' experience with the brand? What nonessential elements can I jettison?

3. Am I better in these functions than my competitors, or are they better than me?

4. What combination of outsourcing, alliance building, and in-house contribution will enhance my brand experience?

5. Can I efficiently manage networks of talent and suppliers, contracted sales forces, and licensed retailers?

Brandnet companies are forcing everyone to look more deeply at their customers' emotional experience of their brand. The rewards will go to those leaders who can best make the brand's promise sing across multiple businesses and products.

This article was first published in May 1997.

George Stalk, Jr.

For most companies, branding is about positioning, advertising, packaging, and catchy logos and slogans. Today that's not enough. In fact, we'll  go so far as to say that much of the money and energy spent in those areas is wasted. Branding in today's marketplace is about the total experience a customer has with a product or service. It is about enticing customers, gaining their trust, and making the experience so pleasant that they are proud of their choice and will tell others about it. It aims to create "apostles" instead of "blasters"—former customers angry about inferior quality, poor service, or wasted time.

I was in the market for a vehicle that would be safe and would meet the needs of my busy wife and our children. We narrowed the choice to two sport utility vehicles. I am often out of town on business, so when one dealer promised that if the vehicle broke down he would pick it up immediately and take it in for servicing, my wife was sold.

For the first two months, my wife told everyone she knew how much she enjoyed the vehicle and appreciated the security afforded by the dealer's guarantee. She was a walking brand builder for the manufacturer.

But the first time the vehicle needed service, the dealer failed to keep his promise. He didn't arrange for immediate pickup, nor did he schedule the service appointment promptly. With that single incident, the dealer destroyed the positive feelings my wife and I had about the brand. No amount of advertising, promotion, or affinity events will fix the problem. What's the lesson here?

Many of today's consumers are

- pressed for time
- short of money
- jaded and skeptical
- starved for affinity relationships

They feel they've been let down by their products, services, and shopping experiences—all of which adds up to a classic case of what we call consumer distemper.

Distemper can't be overcome through packaging or claims. Trust has to be earned at each step in the customer's experience with a company. If you were your company's customer, how would you feel about the experience of buying and paying for the product, getting it delivered, using it, and receiving after-sales service? Too many companies understand this chain of experiences only from their own perspective, not the customer's. We call this chain *end-to-end learning* because customers are learning who and what a company really is. They're learning about the company on the basis of what it does, not what it says. That empirical experience is indelible. So a company had better be sure that it knows what it's teaching its customers. Do you know what it's like to be your company's customer?

One Thing Matters—Delivery

Have you ever measured how much time customers are willing to wait for a product or service? Only a few years ago, a half-hour to prepare a meal at home was considered normal for "fast food" offerings. Today, if the food isn't on the table in five minutes or less, it's not fast food. Similarly, a two-week waiting period for vehicle servicing is at least 13 days too long.

People have become far less willing to believe standard brand claims. Bombarded by advertising on television and radio, in the newspapers, at bus shelters, and even on the Internet, consumers are tuning out. When the message does get through, it's usually received with skepticism.

Today's marketplace offers consumers unprecedented choice. They know that in many categories of goods and services, they can buy lower-cost but high-quality private-label products that will meet their performance requirements. In the tradeoff between cost and quality, the *perceived status and confidence* associated with buying a name brand isn't enough to close the sale anymore. The hard-goods retailer Canadian Tire, for example, goes so far as to advertise that its generic products are made by brand-name companies—same quality, same manufacturer, but at a lower price. In short, marketers are losing their ability to appeal to perceptions of proprietary quality.

Yet consumers at all income levels, for instance, are lining up at Starbucks Coffee to part with more than two dollars for a caffè latte when they could get a regular coffee at a more downscale shop for less than a dollar. Why? Well, Starbucks coffee *is* good, but Starbucks has also made the experience of buying coffee extremely pleasant, and customers are rewarding the company with their loyalty. With a European-style café that invites lingering located on practically every busy urban corner throughout the U.S., Starbucks stands out from its competition. It has become a badge of sophistication, affiliation, and connection.

When consumers find a brand they *believe they can trust,* and the experience of using that product or service is satisfying, their loyalty and word-of-mouth support can be invaluable—as they were for my wife's vehicle's brand for a full two months before the dealer let her down.

What consumer distemper means for companies is that now, more than ever, they cannot afford to forget that the customer's *experience* is an integral part of branding. Managing the brand experience is relevant to virtually all companies, whether they believe they have a brand or not. Brand relationships are not confined to consumer products. They exist with hospitals, taxi companies, cleaners, garages, airlines, restaurants, and more. The strength of a brand experience is inextricably linked to every aspect of buying and using a product, not just to the performance of the product itself.

Exhibit 12

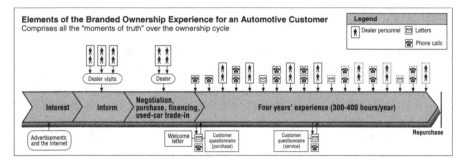

A Single Guiding Vision

Managing a customer's experience is challenging because that experience happens on the company's frontline. In many cases, few employees know firsthand what is happening to customers. More often, managers who make major decisions on new investments or process redesign have little idea of the end-to-end impact their decisions will have on the customer's experience.

Service companies seem to be more aware of the importance of brand experience than packaged goods manufacturers. As early as the 1970s, for instance, Jan Carlzon, head of SAS Airlines, reorganized his company around a concept he called "Moments of Truth." Thirty seconds with an agent at the counter, he discovered, is all it takes for customers to conclude that they're dealing with a great or a lousy airline.

Managing the brand experience requires defining the essence of the customer experience you want to achieve and making sure that everyone, from top to bottom, understands how the brand can influence its customers' daily lives. One client of The Boston Consulting Group has created a series of videos demonstrating its targeted customer experience. These videos are shown not only to marketing managers but also to the systems developers who are building the support infrastructure that will make the experience possible. No written list of systems requirements can ever substitute for the visceral understanding that people develop when they see and hear the customer's experience with the product.

Before launching that next advertising campaign or promotion, ask yourself how your investment decisions affect your customers' experience and whether everyone—from senior executives to counter clerks—is aware of how much the brand's value hinges on the quality of the experience you deliver. Here are some questions to consider:

1. Can you describe the end-to-end experience, through "learn-buy-get-use-pay-service," for different customer segments? Could you present it in a video for employees?

2. Can you measure your ability to overcome the dissatisfactions (such as long waits for delivery and repairs, or inaccuracies in orders and billing) that customers encounter as they progress through their experience of your brand?

3. Can you map the ripple effects of problems from misleading marketing claims to service calls and product returns? Can you measure the economic implication of solving these problems?

4. What is the dollar value of delivering an experience that consistently produces brand apostles and eliminates brand blasters?

5. Can you develop a pilot program and learning environment to analyze how customers respond to the new product or service before you launch other types of branded experiences?

Brand management is at a turning point. As the cacophony of the marketplace escalates, only those brands that deliver will succeed. Increased advertising investment alone won't move the sales needle. Refocus your brand management on the outcomes that matter most—those that affect your customers' lives.

This article was first published in June 1997.

Michael J. Silverstein

I'm waiting in line with my five-year-old son, Charlie, at a fast-food restaurant. It's 1:30 on a Saturday afternoon, and we've "forgotten" to eat lunch. Charlie's hungry and tired from running  errands with me. It's been raining all day, and we're both soaked. Now we've been waiting ten minutes to place our order—seven minutes beyond the industry standard. Finally, I order for Charlie. "Sorry, sir," the salesperson says. "We can give him his meal, but there are no more toys." Five-year-olds understand "no toys," and Charlie begins to wail. For him, this restaurant is about trinkets, not food. In his eyes, its failure to supply the toy has condemned the brand.

It happens every day. Customers are disappointed and even mistreated. Most companies fail to quantify the cost of poor service or to replace it with what we consultants call a "flawless value-delivery system."

Now Charlie doesn't want to go back to that restaurant. Like many dissatisfied customers, he won't risk another disappointment. He is the principal decision-maker in this meal occasion—fast-food lunch—and his preference carries the rest of the family. Moreover, with a life expectancy of more than 70 years, Charlie is worth at least $15,000 in discounted revenues to this restaurant chain—and even more if he grows up to become a "group influencer" or the head of a large household.

Unfortunately, like most companies that disappoint customers, this restaurant chain will never ask Charlie about his visit. Nor will it log the ten-minute wait. Or the out-of-stock toy. Or the lost sale. In fact, when managers look at total sales for that particular Saturday, they may very well conclude that the toy offering was a success.

The Total Brand Experience

A handful of innovative companies are pioneering a different way of going to market. They are focusing on customers' *experience* with their brand and on building a reputation for pleasing them with flawless products or services. They are training their sales associates to understand that nothing less than impeccable performance is acceptable and that bonuses, promotions, and shared profits will be based on rigorously quantified results.

These pioneers understand that their brand's perceived value hinges on what happens before and after the purchase. They realize that word-of-mouth advocacy is worth more than millions of dollars in advertising. They are teaching their organizations that the brand experience begins with the customer's awareness, grows in discussions with friends, blossoms when the customer visits the store and goes through the inform-compare-and-purchase cycle, and persists through use, disposal, and repurchase.

Consider, for example, the fish section of a specialty food store where I shop. Although the supermarkets in the neighborhood all sell good fish for considerably less, this store's fish department has a large and loyal following. The attraction is in the shopping experience, and it begins with the man behind the counter, who lives, breathes, and eats fish.

Every morning, he boasts, he gets to the market before his competitors to select the freshest fish and the largest variety. Back in the store, he doesn't simply push whatever he needs to sell. When customers ask for advice, he questions them on their taste, their cooking skill, and the occasion for the meal. Then he helps them choose the right fish, cuts it to order, and describes how to prepare it. Often he recommends a private-label marinade that the store sells at an 80 percent profit margin. Finally, he tells customers what to serve with the fish, including wine, salad, and dessert.

Most fish sections in supermarkets lose money or break even at best. But our fish expert drives the specialty store's profitability. The lines are long and the fish isn't cheap, but customers know they're getting a high-quality product, good advice, and excellent service for their money.

This store has discovered what all successful retailers understand: you must know your customers as well as you know your products. Managers of large stores who assume that this level of service can be found only in small shops are making a costly mistake. With technology, training, and dedication, salespeople in department and chain stores could treat all customers as if they were carriage trade.

What Do Customers *Really* Think?

Unfortunately, most of the research tools and satisfaction surveys that managers use to understand how customers rate their brand focus on what managers consider important, not on how customers experience a product. Most large-scale surveys measure frequency of use and ask broad questions about service, sales help, and value, but they can't capture the nuances of customers' feelings. Nor are they detailed enough to pinpoint problems, which usually go unidentified until long after they've eroded market share.

To get to the heart of how customers experience your brand, you need to elicit fleeting impressions and inchoate feelings. You don't do that by asking standard questions but by experiencing the product along with your customers. That means shopping with them and paying attention to what they look at, consider, and touch. It means listening to the questions they ask salespeople and seeing how they react to the answers. Even better, it means meeting them in their homes and offices to understand who they are and how they live.

I recently accompanied the head of a major food manufacturer on a visit to a customer's home. The homeowner at first claimed that she had only one or two packages of the manufacturer's product in her kitchen. But when she hunted down all the packages in her home, she discovered—much to her surprise—that she had dozens stashed away in cupboards all over the house. Why, I asked, was she unaware of how much she actually had? At first she was baffled. But after some probing, I discovered that although she and her family liked the product, she rarely found the occasion to serve it. It didn't come to mind when she thought of the traditional food categories for breakfast, lunch, or dinner.

That insight, which was confirmed in visits to several other homes, led the manufacturer to realize that it needed to do more than make and sell the product. It needed to change how customers perceive the product and to educate them on how and when to use it.

Do It Yourself

Senior managers can't delegate this kind of insight gathering. It takes first-hand experience to understand the interaction between the customer, the product, and the environment; to see how customers' impressions inform their decisions; and to recognize moments of truth. If you know where and when decisions are made, you can offer customers new information to enhance their perceptions of your brand.

The economics of retaining your best customers over a lifetime are compelling. The Boston Consulting Group's research into purchasing patterns suggests that acquiring new customers generally costs four to ten times the margin of their first purchase. And, of course, not all customers stay. Those who do, however, usually become "apostles"—word-of-mouth champions who can drive hundreds of units at the highest profit levels.

To create a flawless brand experience, you have to tear down the barriers between your organization and your customers. This means you must

- map your customers' current purchase/use cycles

- identify areas for improvement

- design a better process, including specific steps to make every contact flawless

- measure performance customer by customer

- instill your vision of perfection in all your associates and reward excellent performance

Almost a century ago, Frederick Winslow Taylor, the father of operational effectiveness, asked his hourly iron workers whether they were satisfied with $1.15 per day or whether they aspired to make more money. Taylor was offering them $1.85 for a 300 percent increase in productivity. To get that increase, he gave his workers step-by-step instructions on how to deliver 47 tons per day. These included exacting specifications, continuous advice, daily feedback, and encouragement for achieving the goal. Now Taylor's operational challenge has moved from the factory floor to the consumer frontline. Today's productivity measure has become customer satisfaction and intent to repurchase.

Getting close to customers takes time and effort, but the lifetime value of a customer who is always delighted and never disappointed is well worth it—to you, your organization, and your customers.

This article was first published in August 1998.

George Stalk, Jr.

In a tough competitive environment, managing brands the traditional way—that is, having a good product, making a strong claim, and communicating the message aggressively through advertising and promotions—is no longer enough. To succeed, a company must redefine the promise of its brand to include the reliable delivery not just of a valuable product, or even of an image, but of a total experience. That experience begins the moment a consumer learns about the brand and includes all aspects of shopping for it, purchasing it, using it, getting it serviced, and purchasing it again. To fulfill the brand's promise, company leaders today must become *total brand managers*. What would that role entail? Take a look at the job description below.

Help Wanted: CEO as Total Brand Manager

Role: Grow the brand's profitability by managing the consumer's brand experience from beginning to end. Live the brand, experience it every day, and drive the organization to your level of commitment. Learn. Change. Invest. Renew.

Responsibilities: Control all processes that affect the consumer's brand experience. Set funding and performance targets. Continually improve the brand's value. Protect the brand from get-rich-quick schemes and other misguided promotional ploys.

Requirements: Passion and skill for learning directly from consumers. The ability to experiment and to learn from failure. A belief in fixing what isn't yet broken. Openness, intelligence, intuition, discipline, honesty.

Compensation: A generous share of the value you create over the next five to ten years of your committed and passionate love affair with the brand.

The New Brand Management

Traditional brand managers tend to be junior members of the marketing department. They are responsible mainly for managing promotions, advertising, and relations with the trade. They are more interested in today's bump than tomorrow's crash. They have neither the authority nor the skills to articulate the strategic, cross-functional, long-term perspective that total brand management requires. In fact, in most large companies *no one* is minding the brand.

It takes someone with central authority in the corporation to manage the consumer's experience with the brand. Whether it's the CEO or a very senior executive, that person must have the power, skills, perspective, and access to information necessary to drive not only the development of new products but also the design of new business processes for delivering them. Only the CEO or a senior executive can make judgment calls about funding, give direction to development and delivery functions, and hold managers accountable for hitting their targets. Once the broad brand-management role is safely in senior managers' hands, marketing managers are free to focus on their most important job: managing the relationship with the customer.

What might the new brand-management function look like? Consider Exhibit 13, which indicates that total brand management must encompass three crucial roles.

Brand Management. Brand managers identify the issues to explore with consumers about their brand experiences, and they build the research capa-

Exhibit 13

The Levels of Total Brand Management

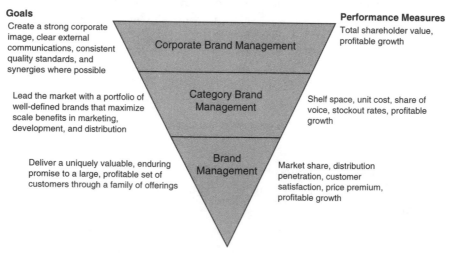

Goals

Create a strong corporate image, clear external communications, consistent quality standards, and synergies where possible

Lead the market with a portfolio of well-defined brands that maximize scale benefits in marketing, development, and distribution

Deliver a uniquely valuable, enduring promise to a large, profitable set of customers through a family of offerings

Corporate Brand Management

Category Brand Management

Brand Management

Performance Measures

Total shareholder value, profitable growth

Shelf space, unit cost, share of voice, stockout rates, profitable growth

Market share, distribution penetration, customer satisfaction, price premium, profitable growth

bilities to gather that intelligence. Then, with help from each of the company's functions—product development, manufacturing, marketing, and sales—they translate this learning into specifications for product development and process design. They also fund the development of brand-building capabilities and track the performance of the functions they oversee.

Category Brand Management. Category managers patrol the boundaries between and the relationships among a company's brands. Category management is becoming increasingly important for two reasons. First, any successful brand manager is going to work unceasingly to expand the brand's scope. He or she will always be scanning the horizon for new line extensions to improve sales growth, expand shelf-space presence, and get more leverage with the trade. If left unchecked, however, such expansion increases the likelihood of overlaps with other brands in the company's portfolio. The category manager must make sure that line extensions don't compete with similar brands in the portfolio.

But category managers play a second and even more important role: managing investments across a coherent brand portfolio. Financing the massive buildup in new capabilities that total brand management requires can rarely be sustained by one brand alone. Therefore, companies need to spread their investments over many brands, cascading across price points and channels.

Corporate Brand Management. When brands become business systems, the corporation itself becomes a kind of brand. For that reason, probably the most important role in total brand management is, strictly speaking, not a functional role at all. It is corporate brand management, which is intimately linked to a company's overall strategy. That's why at some of the best branded-goods companies, the corporate brand manager is the CEO.

Corporate brand management focuses on defining and communicating what the company as a whole stands for, which includes the promise that a long-term relationship with the company is worthwhile. Defining that promise can range from articulating the company's high-level values to detailing companywide standards for service, warranties, and quality.

Total brand management is the essence of the Four Seasons hotel chain's success, since 80 percent of its earnings come from managing hotels rather than owning the hotels that bear its name. CEO Isadore Sharp believes that a successful brand experience is rooted in how he and his senior managers treat the people who deliver that experience. "If you trust people," he says, "they go beyond what is expected of them." At Four Seasons hotels, laundry rooms are often air-conditioned, and employee cafeterias can look as attractive as commercial establishments. Because the company goes an extra step for its staff, the staff goes an extra step for customers. In a well-known anecdote, a maitre d' lent his tux (altered by an on-the-spot seamstress) to a guest who had arrived for a black-tie affair without the appropriate attire.

Corporate brand managers are also responsible for deciding when and how to leverage the brand's equity across other products and businesses. Howard Schultz, CEO of Starbucks Coffee, believes that new products signal a company's commitment to innovation and self-renewal. Before branching out into ice cream, CDs, and other products, however, he insisted that the brand first establish its word-of-mouth reputation for high-quality coffee.

Interestingly, Schultz initially thought that a proposed new product—a milk-shake-like coffee drink—was not at all in keeping with his original concept of a European-style coffee shop. But he was smart enough to listen to his customers, who had been asking for a cold, creamy drink for hot weather. As it turns out, Frappuccino was named one of the best products of the year by *Business Week,* and it garnered 7 percent of the company's total annual revenues in its first year. Schultz calls turning down Frappuccino the "best mistake I never made."

Developing Total Brand Managers

Few companies have CEOs with the broad cross-functional and general management skills that total brand management requires. And even if a CEO has those skills, he or she can't do it all alone. Brand-committed CEOs need brand-committed senior managers with complementary skills. One venerable global marketer has recently determined that its gap in brand-management skills is the biggest obstacle to growth that the company has faced in the past decade.

How are companies filling that gap? Some organizations without a strong tradition of brand management are hiring talented people from traditional packaged-goods companies. Other companies are moving country managers into senior brand-management slots. But the most sophisticated companies are developing more comprehensive approaches.

One global company recently created a multifaceted strategy for nurturing senior brand managers. The company began by designating a new senior vice president position responsible for executive training. It then established career tracks across functions, geographies, and brands to give managers the range of experience they would need to become senior brand managers. At the same time, the company lengthened the tenure of junior brand-management positions from a minimum of 18 months to four or five years.

But the company's most creative move was to develop a portfolio of managerial learning experiences called Action Learning Programs. Designed to enhace on-the-job training, the programs put teams of managers to work solving existing business problems. A manager spends anywhere from two days a week to an intensive three months working on a project before moving to his or her new position. The company actively tracks the results of the projects and uses its findings to improve future programs.

Finally, the company developed a skills database, which describes the range of skills needed for various jobs, and an employee performance database, which tracks the skills that employees exhibit. That information helps match managers with jobs and identify where skill gaps remain—for individuals and for the organization as a whole.

*   *   *

Today's total brand manager must have a holistic perspective on the consumer's experience and on the entire business system that defines a brand. The necessary levels of investment are higher. So are the necessary levels of managerial expertise. As a result, the stakes involved in launching, maintaining, and evolving a brand are much higher today than they were in the past.

But if the risks are high, so are the potential payoffs. In a world where products, markets, channels, and industry boundaries are in flux, a well-managed brand can be the one source of stability, strategic direction, and competitive advantage. It can provide entrée to new markets, new product segments, and entirely new businesses. And the brand manager will take pride of place in the strategic councils of the corporation.

This article was first published in July 1999.

Rolf Bixner, Jim Hemerling, and Rob Lachenauer

Brand value need not be an accident. It can be deliberately created in a process that is objective and measurable. That process involves a quantitative framework, methodology, and language that the whole organization can adopt. Brand managers *can* control *every* aspect of how consumers perceive their brands.

Of course, managing brands for value also requires insight, creativity, and enthusiastic champions. But without hard numbers to justify them, important brand-building investments often lose out to more rigorously defended cost and quality projects.

The Boston Consulting Group's brand-value creation (BVC) technology brings art and science together. It does so by separating brand value into its component parts so that managers can understand *and quantify* its sources and results. BVC makes the process by which brand value is generated explicit, and managers can use that knowledge to increase their company's shareholder value.

From Art to Science: How BVC Works

BVC is based on a simple framework that shows how brand strategy and its drivers (such as products and services, trade programs, communication, and all activities that enhance the customer relationship) affect brand equity (the consumer's perception of the brand and its impact on purchasing behavior). The framework then helps brand managers determine the relationship between brand equity and the brand value that is captured in the market. (See Exhibit 14.)

We measure brand value by

- increases in the price premium (people pay more for it)

- increases in sales volume (people buy more of it)

- brand extensions (brand value transferred to other products)

Implementing BVC is a four-step process. Here is a brief description of each step, followed by comments from some of our clients.

1. Qualitative Assessment. The first taks for brand managers is to understand, qualitatively, how the elements of the BVC framework relate to one another.

Exhibit 14

Brand Value Creation Framework

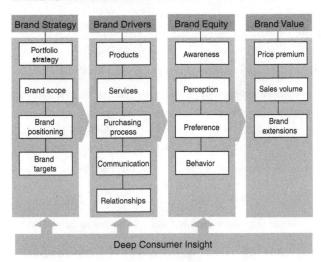

Then they can furnish the framework with empirical data (usually available off the shelf) that are specific to the company and its competitive environment. A side benefit of gathering the data is that it forces managers to discover all the elements that go into creating brand value. This enables them to assess how well the current brand strategy is succeeding in its competitive environment.

Client: Plugging in the right numbers was the first big challenge of the project. We had some heated debates to determine which variables (for example, product functionality, price, or service offerings) were most important to track—not just for our own brands but for those of our competitors as well. And the more competitors' brands we included, the more robust our framework became. Eventually we came up with at least 45 discrete variables, but there could have been hundreds. It was a real learning process—it called our attention to aspects of our service and products that we had never given much thought to.

2. Brand Audit. Once the framework is filled in with the right data, managers can run the audit. This involves two kinds of analysis: measuring the difference between the brand and its competitors in each of the variables, and determining how significant each variable is to the brand's ultimate value. A number of sophisticated analytical tools are available for running the audit. Cross correlation analysis will help to distill large sets of variables into smaller sets. Cluster and factor analyses can identify logical groupings among several variables. Linear regression analysis will determine the relationship between drivers and equity, and between equity and value. The result is a clear chart that the whole organization can understand. It shows how important each variable is to the brand's value and where, in each of those variables, the brand stands in relation to the market leader. (See Exhibit 15.)

Client: The audit really opened our eyes. After we ran the analysis, it was obvious, in hard numbers, which drivers were working and which ones weren't, which ones mattered a lot and which ones didn't. And there were a few surprises.

For instance, one of the first pieces of data that hopped off the page was that two relatively minor competitors—brands that we never worried much about—had been rising

Exhibit 15

Value Gap Analysis Identifies the Need for Action

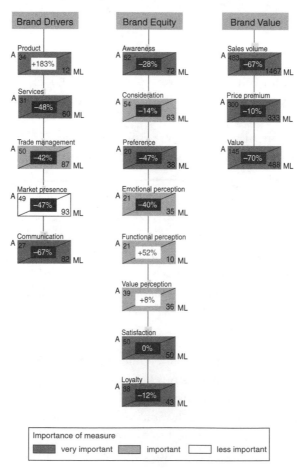

in value at a surprisingly rapid pace for the past three years. The audit also showed that those competitors had accomplished this by increasing their volume and price premiums simultaneously. During the same period, one of our better brands increased its volume but not its premium, and therefore performed less well against its competitors.

We also discovered that another brand had been creating value in some country markets but losing value in others. This exercise was a real eye opener into how our strategy affected our brands in light of the competitive environment within each country. The data clearly showed that the mix of brand value drivers should be tailored to each country's local market.

3. Strategy Development. The next step brings the framework's quantitative results and implications to the organization's senior managers and brand leaders so that they can revise brand strategies or devise altogether new ones. Such a process could involve restructuring the brand portfolio or developing new drivers for selected brands. The managers might also need to dig deeper into some insights before they can determine the right strategies.

Client: We had a number of skeptics in the organization—people with strong functional backgrounds—who didn't believe there was sufficient value in trying to create strong brands. Our audit helped to convince them that competitors' brands in our very own categories were getting ahead of us. It also demonstrated the contributions our people had to make to help us compete. The methodology got everyone focused on value creation—not in a vacuum but within our specific competitive environment. It gave us a context for the targets we had to set for each of the brands and a common language to communicate the required strategies. And it prepared us for the last step.

4. Turning Strategy into Action. Finally, the organization is ready to act on the new strategy. But from this point on, each action will be rigorously measured against the quantitative brand-value framework. The brand-value metrics are also tied to management processes and the incentive system, and new ways of tracking brand value are set up to run continuously. Yet because the BVC process—as well as its language—has become institutionalized across the whole organization throughout all four phases, it isn't as onerous as it might have been.

Client: Now that we were all looking at the same numbers, speaking the same language, and agreeing on our goals, we could go back to our strategy and redirect it to new targets. For one brand, we had to increase brand value where we had been destroying it. To do that, we had to increase volume, which meant setting new targets for improved marketing and pricing strategies. For another brand, we had to increase both volume and price by marketing it to higher-end consumers.

The BVC process helped us become a much more brand-focused organization. By the time we were finished, we had changed our whole strategy: from portfolio objectives down to individual decisions about consumer targets, brand positioning, and innovation.

Brand Value Creation in Action

Why is a rigorous analysis of brand value so important today? Consider the case of a world leader in consumer goods. Its best-known brand enjoyed exceptionally high awareness and solid loyalty—brand equity that had taken generations to create. In recent years, however, the brand's value was beginning to erode. While the company was managing to maintain sales volume, it was losing the price premium it had once enjoyed.

No one had a clear answer for why this was happening. Eventually a committee decided that the brand's image had grown stale, so funds were pumped into a series of high-volume, edgy television commercials. The campaign failed miserably. Not only did the brand *not* regain its price premium a year later, it began to lose sales volume as well.

Growing more concerned, the company sought a remedy in a new service initiative to increase both customer and trade satisfaction. However, because not everyone agreed on the plan, it never got off the ground. One group argued that service was irrelevant because the product's quality was very good. What was needed, they believed, was a new product launch to bring back the excitement. Another group thought the answer lay in improved trade relations and more active trade partnerships. Not surprisingly, the brand continued to fade.

The transformation of the company began with a refocusing on the consumer—new insights, a new customer segmentation, and a new brand promise and positioning—all within the context of a redefined brand portfolio. But then the company had to decide how best to deploy the brands in its different world markets—how much it should invest in different brand drivers in different geographies. This time, thanks to the BVC framework, management had a common language and hard numbers to justify its choice of brand investments.

The whole process was driven by senior management, which allowed the company to move quickly on its insights, even when they differed from long-standing beliefs. Early results are positive: the company's brands are increasing in value faster than the competition's in those countries where BVC has been instituted. Indeed, BVC has become the cornerstone of the company's future strategy.

The Benefits of BVC

Many companies fail to realize the full potential of their brands because they invest in the wrong drivers, at the wrong time, in the wrong sequence. Brand-value creation helps companies recognize the brand dynamics of individual actions within their business system so that they can decide which ones add incremental value and are worthy of investment.

These five questions will help you assess your need for hard numbers in your brand-value creation efforts:

1. Do we know the brand value of each of our brands by market and category, and how it has changed over time?

2. Have we made an explicit decision to drive for premium or volume, or both, in each of our brands?

3. Are all the drivers we have aligned behind our brands performing as expected, and how do we know—by gut feel or hard evidence?

4. Do we know the impact of each brand investment on brand equity and value?

5. Are our brand metrics the right ones and are they hard-wired into our organization?

Brand-value creation is not an "expert system," intended to replace creative thinking or management judgment. It can't forecast market share or revenues. Rather, it helps brand managers understand what consumers value most and how well brands deliver it. BVC provides a method of linking qualitative insights to quantitative measures in every aspect of the complex system that constitutes a brand. It brings together the art and science of brand management in a way that allows brand decisions to reflect the best of both worlds.

This article was first published in November 1999.

Part Six

E·COMMERCE

Thierry Chassaing, Matthew A. Krentz, and William J. Meurer

The Internet has become the equivalent of a boomtown in the days of the Wild West. Wall Street and the venture capitalists have caught gold-rush fever, investing billions on little more than a hope and a prayer.

Like everyone else, branders and retailers feel pressured to join the stampede. Many are reacting to a competitive threat: efficient on-line marketers will capture their most profitable customers. Others see opportunity: manufacturers hungry to extract retailer margins can bypass traditional channels and pocket the retailer's profit. Amid all the hype and hysteria, no one seems quite sure where they're going. All they know is that they don't want to be left behind.

Yet for all its promise, much of the current on-line activity has been uninspiring. Most marketers have merely repackaged existing material to offer limited choice and ho-hum entertainment value. So far, most of the competitive threats have been equally empty.

A GRP Is Not a GRP

A GRP (gross rating point) on the Internet is not the same as one on television. The Internet is for dialogue, building relationships, and bundling products and service. GRP chasers should stay away. True on-line opportunities lie in sales, services, and developing relationships—not in traditional advertising. The value equation, however, has not changed in virtual reality: added customer value plus lower costs equals increased sales, share, and profit.

Instead of creating banner ads and ponderous home pages, vanguard on-line players are using the new channels to provide new services. Their model for winning is based on five rules.

1. **Segment.** Meet the service needs of a clear target segment.

2. **Substitute.** Increase sales by drawing target customers away from other channels and suppliers.

3. **Simplify.** Make the purchase decision easier by providing better and more accessible information.

4. **Enhance value.** Save the user time, money, and effort.

5. **Learn.** Establish a dialogue with individual customers and use the interaction to broaden the knowledge base.

Realizing this vision requires more than nifty games on a Web site. Ambitious on-line marketers will need sophisticated new skills in interface design, information management, and network navigation, and they'll have to upgrade those skills continually. They'll also need the flexibility to respond to the changing economics of different media channels. And finally, they'll have to think in terms of the value equation, which is about satisfying needs, not just selling products.

Looking for Gold On-Line: The First Generation

Some companies will be able to balance that equation more readily than others. Consider information products, such as theater tickets or airline reservations. Since electronic order and delivery can be easier, quicker, and cheaper, traditional retail channels will be particularly vulnerable to competition. Today, travel agents earn roughly 10 to 20 percent of an airline ticket's cost for booking the flight and printing the ticket. On-line software now on the market allows travelers to check flight information, availability, and pricing on their own across multiple airlines 24 hours a day. For the airlines, however, such software is a mixed blessing: although the airlines will save on the commissions they formerly paid to travel agents, their customers will be better equipped to shop for the best deals.

Home shopping, including home delivery, can pose a significant challenge. Food retailers have been experimenting with this opportunity for decades, few with success. Perhaps the longest-running electronic grocery service is Télémarket, operating on France's Minitel system. Though it has survived where others have gone under, after ten years of operation it has reached neither critical mass nor adequate profit performance.

Peapod, a home-shopping grocery service in Boston, Chicago, and San Francisco, has been able to correct some of the customer interface problems of the Télémarket system. Télémarket, for instance, has no memory, which means orders have to be reentered every time. Peapod offers an on-line shopping environment that is much more user-friendly, with a memory and point-and-click technology. Products are listed by category, making them easy to find, and customers can sort by brand, supplier, price, and even fat levels.

Peapod can cut shopping time by two-thirds. Not surprisingly, it has captured nearly 80 percent of its customers' total shopping bill, while average grocers take only 40 percent. Peapod's prices, however, remain substantially above those in the local market. If it can't trim its premium, Peapod will remain a specialty service for relatively young, affluent, time-starved consumers willing to pay for convenience.

Finding Gold On-Line: The Second Generation

As a first-generation electronic retailer, Peapod satisfies about three and a half of the five rules for on-line success: it enhances value, at least for affluent customers, and it segments, substitutes, and simplifies. But with its relatively high costs, it fails to offer mass-market value, and it has done little with the information it gets from customers. Amazon.com, an electronic bookstore with more than one million books, is a second-generation on-line marketer. It has started to deliver on all five rules.

Amazon.com serves a specific target audience; entices it away from traditional bookstores; simplifies the purchase decision by enabling users to search for books by author, subject, or title; enhances customer value with offers such as a discount on all books reviewed in the latest *New York Times Book Review*; and learns from its constant communication with customers.

Through continuous e-mail contact, the electronic bookstore can flag new releases and recommend books on the basis of individual preferences. In turn, customers can contribute book reviews, enter contests, and engage in on-line conversations with publishers and authors. Without stores or clerks, the company knows the interests and tastes of each of its customers.

Amazon.com has also put its on-line economics to work. With a single warehouse replacing numerous individual stores, it saves space costs (rent, maintenance, utilities), store costs (cashiers and stock keeping), and handling costs (no double handling of products between the warehouse and stores). While a conventional bookstore turns its inventory about 4 times a year, Amazon.com turns its products 150 times.

Although it employs fewer than 50 people, Amazon.com reaches nearly everywhere. In less than a year (and entirely through word of mouth), it has become a global business with a small but growing customer base drawn from more than 60 countries. In a recent interview in *PC Week*, Bill Gates explained that he buys his books from Amazon.com because "time is short, and they have a big inventory, and they've been very reliable."

Not Too Early, Not Too Late

The electronic marketplace is developing rapidly, and trends in demographics and technology suggest the pace will only accelerate. So far, however, marketers are underestimating what it takes to seize technology-driven opportunities. They rush in too early and spend too much on what amounts to too little. They merely graft another advertising channel onto their marketing mix. Instead, they should be thinking strategically about how they can lower their total costs by using on-line channels to change their core operations and offer better services.

Whether competition or opportunity is driving your on-line ambitions, can you answer the questions below with a definite "yes"?

- Do I understand the economic implications of the technology for the entire business system?

- Do I understand how the technology will entice customers to buy more, and more customers to buy?

- Do I have a plan to begin a dialogue with my customers and create a lifelong monogamous relationship?

- Do I have the right people to execute the five rules for finding gold on-line?

This article was first published in October 1996.

BRANDING ON THE INTERNET: NAVIGATING AROUND THE HYPE

Dennis Goldstein, Richard Lesser, and Miki Tsusaka

Today, all but a few major brands have a presence on the Web. It is expected that by the year 2000, close to half a billion dollars will have been  spent on Internet advertising. Unfortunately, most marketers have taken the Web plunge without seriously considering its benefits or its applicability to their products. When budgets come up for review, they can't document a payback to justify reinvestment. A combination of hype, competition, and fear has resulted in impulsive investments and poor returns. Many marketers are now beginning to ask the questions they should have addressed before they entered cyberspace.

- Do we really have to make these investments at rapidly escalating rates?

- What are we getting from our site today and how do we improve our return?

- How do we learn to recognize new electronic branding opportunities and get more from them?

- Can we earn back the costs of connecting with our target?

A corporate Web site is not for everyone. It is ideal for offering detailed product information that supports a purchase decision. It can be highly efficient for providing postpurchase support. It has the potential to deepen relationships with loyal or highly involved customers. But it is difficult to use a Web site to create new demand or win broader exposure. Today the task of turning cyberspace into a vehicle for building brand image is extremely challenging.

For some companies, the Web is unquestionably the right place to be, and the sooner they start up the learning curve, the better. Many others would be wise to curtail their spending, apply the funds to other vehicles, monitor the competition, and wait. Most consumer goods companies, however, fall somewhere in the middle. For them we recommend a cautious advance, armed with a rigorously focused strategy based on

- clear objectives

- a platform for learning and experimentation

- branding tools appropriate for the medium

- hard metrics and action triggers

- a plan for phased investment

Who's Out There?

Today, more than 20 percent of adults in the U.S.—that's 40 million people—use the Internet, the World Wide Web, or both. As search vehicles become easier to use, the audience is becoming increasingly mainstream in age, income, and education.

The time people spend on the Internet doesn't come out of nowhere. Most often it is taken from television, radio, newspapers, and magazines. Therefore, if companies continue to advertise only through traditional channels, they risk losing a significant portion of their most affluent audience as Net usage grows. Beating the odds for success on the Net, however, will take careful planning to offer real value where visitors can easily find it.

The best Web sites are content sites that provide real value in transactions, services, or information and that help to strengthen the bond between manufacturers and consumers. Billboard sites with little to offer beyond fun and games don't justify their costs. Such promotional sites may garner "hits," but those contacts don't automatically translate into increased sales, or even return visits.

Getting Attendance and Attention

Surfing the Net isn't like flipping through a magazine. Users descend from large general categories to specific sites. Suppose you make facial tissues and hope to attract hay-fever sufferers by offering advice on allergies. Your target audience is more likely to stop at a site for allergy sufferers than one belonging to a paper-products manufacturer. Therefore, you'd be better off affiliating with a site that addresses the customer's need.

If you do decide to start a site, begin by establishing whether you want to achieve reach or repeat visits. If your objective is broad reach, you'll need an aggressive strategy to attract visitors. If your objective is repeat visits, you'll need compelling content that is updated regularly. Unlike traditional advertising, in which the message is "pushed" to the audience on billboards, on television, and in magazines, the Web has to "pull" its audience by creating reasons for them to want to visit. As yet, no Web site can reach out and claim a prospect's attention against his or her will—not even for a fraction of a second.

In fact, the Net is replete with expensive sites that are little more than retrofit print ads. Unlike radio, print, and TV ads, which attract viewers with the articles and programs that surround them, the sites on the Net must not only be interesting in themselves but offer a reason to go there.

Automakers, for instance, attract potential customers with detailed, customized information on product bundles, dealer locations, and pricing. But what if the product or the buying process isn't complicated enough that people welcome supplemental information about it? Well, maybe the product's environment is. A hiking-boot company, for example, might have a Web site that offers trail maps, expedition advice, and nature reports. The point is that in a *seek-me-out* environment you'll need more than fancy graphics and wild colors to attract and hold an audience.

Interactive Web sites allow you to probe target customers about when, where, and why they need certain products so that you can present the product at the right time and place. The Net offers the opportunity to go beyond broad advertising in developing relationships with consumers. Its interactivity and comparatively low cost per contact will eventually enable manufacturers to customize the brand experience and create deeper bonds with consumers. A baby-food manufacturer, for example, could offer nutritional advice, on-line experts, and chat rooms for parents. It could also provide information and offerings tied to specific stages of a baby's development.

Look Before You Leap

To reap these benefits, you've got to do your homework. Value from the Internet comes from incremental increases in volume achieved through new customers, more frequent purchases, higher-margin customers, and loyal customers. It also comes from new revenue streams and more efficient product delivery (fewer handlings, less inventory, lower markups). But you need to be explicit about where you will extract this value.

Most important, don't take the plunge without carefully mapping your consumer segments. Ask yourself:

- What consumers do we want to attract?

- What economic value can we create for these consumers?

- Do we try to reach as many of them as possible? Do we give them a reason to come back? Do we give them a reason to show up at all?

- What messages should we be sending, and how will those messages lead to profits?

- Are we capturing insights that will allow us to learn and grow as the technology and user base evolve?

If you want to attract new customers and people who wouldn't ordinarily seek you out, and if you are going to invest time and resources in the Net, then do it right. Make sure that your site is compelling, that it satisfies unmet needs for the consumers you want to attract, and that you build it in a logical part of the Internet neighborhood.

You can aspire to be creative, clever, and bold on the Net, but unless your site brings increasing value to you and your customers, you'd be better off investing your resources elsewhere.

This article was first published in August 1997.

SERVING THE E-GENERATION

David C. Edelman, Carlos Bhola, and Andrew Feiler

Reprinted with permission from *Marketing News,* published by the American Marketing Association, "Keeping Up with the E-Generation," David C. Edelman, Carlos Bhola, Andrew Feiler, September 1, 1997, Vol. 31.

A new force is emerging in our society. It is the e-generation. Already shaping our on-line environments, its members are transferring their expe-

riences in cyberspace to form their expectations for every-day life. Increasingly they demand rapid response, easy access, and a sense of control. Companies that seamlessly connect with the e-generation through both on-line and conventional channels will create tomorrow's successful brands.

It's About Time

The e-generation is defined not by demographics but by a common set of experiences. On-line usage spans all age groups and Web site content—from Disney to ESPN to AARP. The e-generation is not synonymous with Generation X.

While on-line users are highly attractive by the standards of traditional demographics (surveys suggest that more than half are professional, more than two-thirds have at least a college education, and almost half have household incomes in excess of $50,000), the most powerful behavioral dimension for understanding the e-generation is time sensitivity. Surveys consistently show that saving time, in terms of convenience and efficiency, is the leading reason consumers use on-line capabilities. Faster modems and services are cited as the primary means for stimulating greater on-line usage.

Yes, some e-generation members linger in cyberspace. These *surfers,* typically the young and the elderly, have more available time. They tend to be entertainment-oriented, and they demand freshness and richness in their on-line content. While on-line efforts often focus on these surfers, we think selling products and services to those with less time may be more profitable. The *instant-gratification seekers* are less interested in entertainment than in accomplishing what they want to quickly.

It's About *Fatness* and *Stickiness*

As companies use on-line channels to improve timeliness and convenience, they are finding that cross-selling opportunities are emerging. The best way to enhance a transaction is to have all the information about the customer's past purchases, credit profile, preferred payment mechanism, and so forth, close at hand. By leveraging information provided by customers, businesses are increasing the fatness and stickiness of their customer relationships. Several strategies are emerging that allow marketers to exploit on-line capabilities while catering to customers' time sensitivity.

Give customers a return on their information investment. Having information about an individual's preferences or other personal information can be an extremely powerful tool. It can help a business shape offers and increase efficiency in targeting. Many companies are striking a new bargain with on-line consumers: in exchange for more personal information, they are providing enhanced value. Greet Street, an on-line greeting-card company, for example, asks customers to register their card-giving occasions. By knowing to whom customers need to send a card, for which occasions, and what they have sent in the past, Greet Street is able to send e-mail reminders of upcoming events. It can also suggest customized cards for each occasion.

Make buying effortless. By saving transaction data from past purchases, marketers can reuse the data to facilitate future purchases. By calling 1-800-FLOWERS, for example, consumers can select flowers from a ready-made list, then provide the rest of the information to complete the transaction. Compare this with the time it would take to go to a flower store, select a bouquet, choose and sign a card, and then deliver the gift. By exploiting technology's ability to save and reuse information, a growing number of services are finding ways to streamline the buying process and reduce the stress of what most people think of as running errands.

Integrate what was previously disjointed. Until recently, AT&T customers needed to keep track of their own various telephony and financial services accounts with AT&T. They received separate statements from each business unit and had to sort through myriad options to determine the "rewards" they were being offered. Through its Web site, AT&T True Rewards now integrates the loyalty programs available across AT&T's business units. One change of address, one change of credit card number. One place to see all points, one place to redeem them. By enticing customers to let AT&T True Rewards manage an ever broadening array of information, AT&T is securing tight relationships and the opportunity to be the preferred provider of new services.

Give customers more control. To determine the status of an order, many service providers still require customers to speak directly to an account representative. Waiting—first on hold to get an account representative, and then while he or she tracks down the order—takes time and patience. By contrast, Federal Express allows its customers to bypass the human interface by providing package tracking and account information through the Web. Because this information is also available through telephony channels, FedEx customers can access information about their accounts through their channel of choice and at the time of their choice. Clients have found using the Web so convenient that FedEx has been able to reduce its inbound call volume significantly and, in turn, its customer service head count.

As consumers interact with brands in ways that are information intensive, they are increasingly expecting companies to know more about them and to make doing business easier. When consumers have a need, offering solutions is seen not as sales but as an attractive service.

It's About Your Brand

The e-generation rarely interacts with a brand solely in cyberspace. On-line interactions have ripple effects through all channels, thus making on-line strategy a core brand-management issue. Most marketers relegate their on-line strategy development to skunkworks teams or outsource it to cyberagencies. This often leads to an on-line experience that is disconnected from the customer's off-line experience. Customers might telephone about content they saw on a Web site or search the Web for information on an offer that was featured on television. By failing to recognize that on-line customers use multiple channels, marketers risk burdening their service channels with costly additional volume and generating widespread customer dissatisfaction.

As the e-generation grows in size and importance, the biggest challenge for marketers is to extend the capabilities designed for on-line environments across all their customer contact channels and into their overall business systems. Companies that fail to develop rapid response skills and strong information bonds with their customers will find it harder and harder to do business with the e-generation.

David Pecaut

Business success is grounded in the ability to understand where the economy is heading, which products will sell, and how markets will evolve.

But forecasting the future of electronic commerce is especially daunting because the offerings change daily and the market is growing exponentially. Opportunities abound, but no one knows for sure which ones will prove profitable.

Given that uncertainty, companies developing strategy for the Internet should aspire to be *generally correct and not specifically wrong*. That means anticipating, in big-picture terms, where the emerging opportunities will lie but not locking into an inflexible business model or strategic direction. For example, whereas several established media companies made specifically wrong bets on building Internet portals, Yahoo became a leader by guessing correctly that the Internet would be difficult for users to navigate and by changing direction frequently as opportunities arose.

A big challenge in such an environment is to resist the false assumptions that can lead a company astray. Not surprisingly, many myths about electronic commerce have already gained credence. Here are five that are being debunked by the experiences of on-line retailers.

Myth 1. Because the impact of technology and the pace of technological change are unpredictable, companies should wait before doing business on the Internet.

In fact, the pace of technological change is the most predictable part of electronic commerce. Moore's Law, which tells us that computing power doubles every 18 months, has proved true for the past 15 years and will probably remain true for at least another 10. The question, then, is not *if* but *when* those economics will penetrate a company's value chain and how they can create an opportunity.

Myth 2. Only certain products can be marketed and sold on the Internet.

On-line retailing has moved beyond the belief that only standardized products, such as books and CDs, can be sold on the Internet. The reality is that on-line retailers are using a wide variety of business models to sell almost any product or service.

The key to successful on-line retailing is the retailer's ability to leverage the information power and reach of the Internet to create an end-to-end experience that is enjoyable and offers value. Some on-line retailers sell and deliver products directly to customers, as on-line booksellers and computer companies do. Some help consumers navigate the product selection process. Consider Microsoft's CarPoint, which has leveraged the information power of the Internet to help consumers choose a car by allowing them to compare features and examine performance data, quality statistics, and other information. CarPoint then refers those people to local auto dealers to complete the sale. Consumers have embraced this new approach: more than 25 percent of U.S. automobile buyers now use an on-line service to research a purchase.

Myth 3. E-commerce will be a zero-sum game.
Rather than create new markets, so the theory goes, e-commerce will simply shift sales from traditional retail channels to the on-line channel. It is true that the 24-hour-a-day availability of on-line shopping allows time-pressed consumers to make purchases they had deferred. However, on-line retailing can actually increase overall demand for products.

The biggest physical bookstore might have 170,000 titles, but on-line bookstores have 3 million. Furthermore, the leading on-line bookstores, such as barnesandnoble.com and Amazon.com, have become adept at using customers' previous purchases to make recommendations that result in additional sales. Book consumption has increased in North America because of on-line selling. People aren't necessarily *reading* more books, but they certainly are buying more.

Myth 4. All goods and services offered on-line will become commodities.
Some fear that the Internet will drive down prices and force all retailers' product lines to look the same. To be sure, electronic shopping will give consumers unprecedented power to dictate a product's features and price, but it will also be an opportunity for sellers to walk customers upmarket to higher-margin products. Rather than "push" products, the Internet will allow consumers to "pull" the products they want.

Producers should watch very closely as consumers begin to design their own products and climb the price ladder. Dell, for example, has found that computer buyers are inclined to purchase more expensive computers and add more options when they can configure their order directly over the Internet. By understanding the psychology of on-line shopping, marketers can move their customers out of the commodities mentality into a personalized, big-ticket shopping experience.

Myth 5. On-line commerce and off-line commerce are separate worlds.
In fact, some of the most successful on-line retailers blend their on-line and off-line channels. Contrary to popular belief, 59 percent of all on-line retailing revenues in 1998 were generated by retailers who already had an off-line presence.

U.S. discount brokerage Charles Schwab, for instance, has opened 250 branches. The primary purpose of these physical locations is to acquire customers, who are then served by Schwab's telephone and on-line services. And one of the first on-line retailers, 1-800-FLOWERS, is continuing to build flower shops. Why? Because a physical store gives a brand more visibility and attracts people who would not find the company on the Internet.

Companies are also integrating their on-line and off-line channels for advertising and promotions. Canadian Tire, a hard goods retailer, has found that requests for its weekly on-line flier have far exceeded the company's expectations. This form of electronic permission-based direct marketing is driving incremental sales at the company's physical stores.

*　　*　　*

As e-commerce continues to gain ground, the best strategies will aim to fill a latent consumer need—whether it is the need for more convenience, a more customized product, or more options. The massive selection offered by on-line bookstores is meeting the need for choice, convenience, and availability. The on-line car-buying services are satisfying the need for objective information without the pressure-filled atmosphere of a show room.

The most successful on-line sellers also look for anomalies and capitalize on them. Sometimes the best opportunities lie hidden in something consumers are doing that, at first glance, makes no sense. One on-line retailer, for example, noticed a few senior citizens buying rap CDs. Follow-up with those customers revealed an opportunity for a direct marketing program aimed at helping grandparents buy pop music for their grandchildren.

Finally, successful on-line retailers are able to move quickly by not "hardwiring" their business models until they understand the real economic leverage points. Amazon.com began by building its business on Ingram's traditional book-wholesaling infrastructure. But now it is building its own warehouse and logistics system.

In the fast-paced world of e-commerce, retailers must have a deep understanding of consumers and be able to create a rich and rewarding virtual shopping experience. Successful companies will use that knowledge to define and, more important, rapidly refine their on-line business models so that they remain generally correct and never slip into the trap of being specifically wrong.

This article was first published in March 1999.

WINNING ON THE NET: CAN BRICKS-AND-MORTAR RETAILERS SUCCEED ON THE INTERNET?

Joseph C. Davis and Stephen H. Gunby

How many hard-nosed retailers would throw away $30 million? How many would do so in ways that leave their whole company at risk?

Presumably few. Yet virtually every bricks-and-mortar retailer, and some catalogers, are doing just that as they chase the gold of the Internet. Contrary to increasing popular belief, that result isn't a historical inevitability; rather, it is happening as much because retailers are being browbeaten into throwing away solid instincts as it is because they are relying too much on instincts that are irrelevant on the Net.

What's Going On?

The first 24 months of a brick-and-mortar retailer's concentrated attack on the Internet can easily cost in excess of $30 million to build an organization and an effective Web site, and to compete in the race for eyeballs.

Although the sum is considerable and the losses can destroy market value, the investment itself is neither good nor bad. It may well be a reasonable price of admission to the Internet. In fact, it likely is modest compared with the price of admission down the road.

But if past experience is any guide, at the end of 18 to 24 months many retailers will have created

- limited consumer value

- limited opportunities for strategic advantage

- limited benefit (and in some cases harm) to the core brand

- virtually no chance of enduring profitablity

Result: many retailers need to begin again, junking much of the work to date.

This cycle is unnecessary. The economics of sucessful on-line retailers, when you exclude growth-oriented costs, look radically different from those in Exhibit 16. The market has awarded enormous value to these retailers, especially when they can tell a convincing story of long-term competitive advantage.

Exhibit 16

The Cost of E-Commerce

A Typical Pro Forma

($ million)	Year 1	Year 2	Year 3
Net sales	5.0	20.0	100.0
Gross margin	1.7	6.8	34.0
Total expenses	12.2	22.6	81.0
EBIT	–10.5	–15.8	–47.0
Cash flow	–18.5	–22.0	–61.0

So why is it that leading bricks-and-mortar retailers have been laggards in e-commerce? More important, what can be done about it?

Debunking the Dinosaur Theory

One explanation for the current situation, called the dinosaur theory, claims that bricks-and-mortar retailers are a dying breed, too slow and too rooted in the past to survive. According to the theory's exponents, these retailers should either resign themselves to failure or hand over the reins to people who supposedly understand the new climate: usually 20-somethings with no retail experience.

The truth, of course, is more complicated. Succeeding on the Internet is not about throwing away all instincts. In fact, the dismal performance of the bricks-and-mortar retailers on the Net is at least as attributable to the mistakes of managers browbeaten by the dinosaur theory as it is to the attempts of dinosaurs to dance. To succeed on the Internet, bricks-and-mortar retailers will have to uncover and leverage the strengths they have that are relevant to the new medium and combine them with new capabilities.

What to Do?

Venturing onto the Internet, like entering any new business, is a process with multiple stages, each with its own pitfalls (see Exhibit 17). Seven of the most common traps are described below

1. failure to do the essential analytical homework

2. insufficient breadth of vision with respect to potential e-commerce concepts.

3. insufficient breadth of vision with respect to the Internet opportunity beyond e-commerce

4.   delayed attention to fulfillment and customer service

5.   inadequate leveraging of core strengths

6.   organizational inflexibility and too little focus on partnering

7.   failure to build in an aggressive "redefine" stage

Exhibit 17
Developing Breakthrough Concepts for the Internet

Ideation	Concept Development	Concept Realization			Business execution/ modification
		Partner Development	Business Planning	Transition	

Key Activities

Brainstorm hypothesis	Define content	Recruit executives	Roll out
Identify customer value	Develop economic models	Create patrnerships	Monitor market evolution and competitive landscape
• current off-line dissatisfactions	Explore partnership options	Build Web site	
• on-line behaviors		Develop database content	Measure and monitor own performance
		Create marketing strategies and plans	
		Create business plans, targets, and measures	Refine, review, and update

Pitfalls

Economics not understood		Try to do it all alone	Fail to renew offering continually
• cost		Fail to consider requirements for success beyond the site itself, such as	
• value		• customer service	Make tweaks to offering but don't fundamentally rethink
Target consumer not defined		• fulfillment	
Consumer value fuzzy		Invest in site development but don't fully address the need to attract eyeballs	
Source of differentiation unclear		Overvalue banner advertising	Allow competitors to gain advantage through commit- ment to current offering
Price/value relationship ill defined		Fail to create site that generates customer loyalty	
Answer assumed and not rigorously challenged		Consider potential partners too narrowly	Fail to exploit consumer base
Benefit too long-term			

1. Failure to Do the Essential Analytical Homework

"Internet time" isn't just jargon—it's a fair characterization of the pace required to succeed on the Net, which is rapid even by retail standards.

But even in the virtual world, the laws of economics, of customer value, and of competition have not been repealed. Few consumers will want to spend $40 to get a common carrier to deliver an $18 Rubbermaid garbage can to their homes. And although the Internet might allow Starbucks Coffee to increase its value proposition by making it possible for customers to order coffee beans for home delivery, the Internet can't deliver a cup of fresh-brewed coffee. Moreover, simply putting up a Web site does not assure the on-line retailer of traffic generated at a viable cost, nor does it guarantee survival in the face of competitors with scale advantages or a better offering.

Like every channel, the Internet has to deliver *value for money*. The value must be superior to that delivered by other channels and must appeal to *sufficiently large segments of consumers across sufficiently large numbers of SKUs*. For an individual company to make money on the Net, it will have to create value in a way that is *competitively advantaged*.

To succeed on the Net, retailers must understand the core economics of the medium in terms of SKUs, enterprise economics, and customer value. We recommend an approach that we call E-nalysis.[1] (See Exhibit 18.)

Analyzing basic fulfillment economics of SKU can dramatically influence the Internet value proposition. Considering that the costs of order taking, fulfillment, delivery, and returns for a typical UPS order are $6 to $8, many SKUs cannot be sold in usual order sizes at current retail prices and ever

[1] E-nalysis is a service mark of The Boston Consulting Group.

Exhibit 18

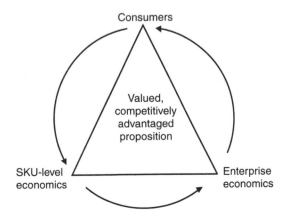

yield a profit. To sell a low-end alarm clock on the Net, for example, a retailer would have to find a large number of consumers willing to pay a premium of 50 percent over the price at a traditional big-box retailer. For a garlic press, the premium is 110 percent; for cat food, 50 percent. On the other hand, a mag wheel can be profitably sold on the Internet for 19 percent *less* than at a traditional outlet; for a bundled order of three CDs, the price is 10 percent less; and for a low-turning book, it is 21 percent less.

Performing basic SKU-level analysis thus drives a company to confront powerful questions: are we trying to sell at a premium? If so, to whom? What value will justify that premium? Will others attack that segment with a better value proposition at a lower price? Do we have a way to avoid a premium and still make money? If so, how? By cherry-picking SKUs that have high value and low fulfillment costs? By encouraging large orders in bundled purchases? By somehow breaking the economics of fulfillment and delivery? Unfortunately, most retailers have neither conducted this analysis nor confronted those questions.

A second area to investigate is enterprise costs. Analysis of the costs of playing on the Internet suggests that, contrary to conventional wisdom, scale will be critical in most retail categories. To survive, small players will have to justify a premium over their large competitors, find superior bundling opportunities, or somehow fundamentally transform the economics of the Web. These scale economics, which are well understood by the leading players, are driving some of the biggest bets currently taking place on the Internet—both enormous investment in marketing costs as well as recent merger-and-acquisition activity, such as CDNow's merger with N2K and subsequent merger with Columbia House. And yet many retailers' plans fail to address these issues adequately.

Most important, to create and sustain a leading position on the Net, a retailer must offer much more consumer value than 24-hour availability and interesting graphics. A 50,000-volume bookstore site, for example, has to have more going for it than the name Wal-Mart to compete against Amazon.com.

The Internet has vast potential to address expressed and latent consumer needs in new ways. The key is to uncover those opportunities and find an economic formula that makes it possible to pursue them in a competitively advantaged way. All retailers that are succeeding on the Net today pass the screen of E-nalysis. Companies that do not subject their thinking to that discipline are at risk.

2. Insufficient Breadth of Vision with Respect to Potential E-Commerce Concepts

Basic E-nalysis reveals a fundamental truth: concepts that make sense in bricks-and-mortar space don't necessarily make the most sense in cyberspace.

Why should they? Many of the traditional limits of space—operating hours and cost-effective availability of product expertise, for instance—are minimized on the Web. But new constraints arise, such as fulfillment economics, the difficulties of interacting with merchandise on the Web, and rapidly changing technologies of bandwidth and graphics. Consider these fundamentally new economics and constraints, why should we assume the traditional bundling of mechandise catagories will prevail?

But most retailers start by asking, How can I get all or part of my current store on the Web?

The realization that winning concepts are likely to be substantially different from the current concept is a jarring one. It raises difficult questions of whether the Internet should support the core or be a business in its own right, an issue that can paralyze a retailer into failure. Success demands early recognition of the issue and constructive discussion.

3. Insufficient Breadth of Vision with Respect to Internet Opportunity Beyond E-Commerce

For most retailers, the natural focus of the Internet is e-commerce. But the Net can, in fact, support an existing bricks-and-mortar business by

- providing information about availability and item reservation, thereby driving traffic to the physical store

- supporting special-order programs

- improving effectiveness through interactive kiosks and training tools

- introducing new approaches to marketing and ways to maximize marketing investments

- supporting supply chain initiatives

- holding e-auctions to eliminate overstocks and returned goods

The e-commerce group usually is not the place to drive all these initiatives. To exploit the full power of the Net, retailers must periodically survey the ways it can help the business and rethink roles and responsibilities within the organization.

4. Delayed Attention to Fulfillment and Customer Service

Following the 1998 Christmas season, the press was full of reports about hiccups in fulfillment and customer service: Internet orders that were never filled, customers who had no idea how to return goods, people returning goods they purchased on-line to a physical store only to be met with blank stares, and executives who spent the holidays packing boxes.

The fundamental operations that support an on-line retailer—individual order taking, picking, packing, and delivery—are different from the operations of most bricks-and-mortar retailers. That fact is beginning to drive some traditional retailers to establish partnerships with or acquire companies that have strong fulfillment and customer service capabilities. Consider Federated's purchase of Fingerhut, Target's acquisition of Rivertown, and Kmart's partnership with On-Demand Solutions.

Whether through acquisitions, licensing, or capability building, bricks-and-mortar retailers must address this issue at the outset or risk alienating customers.

5. Inadequate Leveraging of Core Strengths

No established organization is likely to be as nimble as a start-up. But existing retailers can leverage enormous advantages to overcome their disadvantages. For example, Victoria's Secret's brand and marketing capabilities allowed for the most successful Web site launch to date for a traditional retailer. Other players are cross marketing with great success: they often can acquire customers for one-quarter to one-half the cost of their purely on-line competitors.

The key challenge is organizational: to set up the business and its linkages to the core in ways that leverage strengths while neither detracting from the core nor inhibiting the creation of the on-line business.

6. Organizational Inflexibility and Too Little Focus on Partnering

An aggressive attack on the Internet will likely require capabilities beyond those the retailer already has. It may also require attracting new talent with a different incentive structure. Success, therefore, will depend on substantial organizational agility, a regular rethinking of the organizational form, and a continual search for partners that can help extend the business or help it succeed more quickly.

7. Failure to Build In an Aggressive "Redefine" Stage

The world of the Internet, of course, is changing daily, not just in terms of consumers' perceptions and market values but in reality. New insights into consumers, new launches or counterattacks by competitors, and ongoing technological advances mean rapid changes in opportunities.

Although this climate cannot be used as an excuse to pick any old idea and put it on the Web, it does suggest that the management of all Internet-based activities must include checkpoints and reevaluation along the way—it must be an iterative rather than a linear process.

Will You Succeed?

The above description of the potential pitfalls helps explain why existing retailers have found it difficult to lead in this new field. The problem isn't that they are dinosaurs; it is that they must do nothing less than bring CEO-level insight, judgment, and decision-making abilities to a business that does not yet exist, while continuing to manage an extremely complicated one that does.

And yet retailers have no choice. If they fail to take on these challenges, they risk marginalization. More important, existing retailers can and should win. The capabilities they bring in consumer insight, market power, and cross-marketing skills—harnessed the right way—will yield victory.

This article was first published in August 1999.

Part Seven

GLOBAL MARKETS

Philip Siegel and Michael J. Silverstein

For both retailers and packaged goods companies, the pressure to conquer the world is enormous. It comes from the relentless demand for earnings growth, the slowing growth in domestic markets, and a broad recognition of consumer income growth in Asia, Latin America, and Eastern Europe. For many businesses, the global frontier is no longer an option; it's a necessity. But it's also a land mine.

Few of the majors today have earned back their cost of capital from their massive global spending spree of the last decade. Even fewer have achieved global brand icons. But many have drained their domestic business units of risk-seeking, ambitious managers. And they've created an unsustainable hodgepodge of positions with no priority markets, no best practices, and no systematic price premiums, cost advantage, or preferred brands. Instead, they've bought into local companies with high cost, low quality, and unextendable brands, or they've built from scratch secondary brand positions that bleed red ink.

We believe it's time for exhausted multinationals to step back from the global stampede and create a center-driven, highly orchestrated, meticulously planned global strategy. It's time for fact-based objectives and coordinated marketing strategies. It's time for common metrics, research protocols, and investment guidelines. For the locally focused, profit-deprived international manager, this is a wake-up call to global attention and collaboration.

The Case for Uniformity

To be sure, a tightly centralized global approach is not the answer for every company in every situation. Adaptation to local tastes and practices is sometimes necessary to sell brands in foreign markets. Our experience in working with multinationals, however, has convinced us that many companies give up the vision of a truly global brand too easily—and for reasons that have more to do with internal obstacles than external realities.

Customizing the product can compromise the brand's integrity, its long-term cost position, and its growth consistency. Unnecessary local concessions, we believe, are at the heart of the problems many global companies are having today. If this sounds as if it could be happening to you, it's time to take a good hard look at your global strategy and the beliefs on which it is based.

In a nutshell, the argument for local accommodation goes something like this: "Only a super-brand, single-product company with the universal recognition of a Coca-Cola or a McDonald's can override local tastes, habits, and markets. Lacking such a brand, a company must adapt its offering and systems to the local environment." The problem with this argument is that this strategy is often a self-fulfilling prophecy. A company may lack a strong global brand because of local compromises it has already made.

Many well-known, moderately successful global companies tailor their products to local markets. They have different brand names in different locations, different packaging, sourcing, advertising, ingredients, and price points. A product may be the premium brand in one market but not in others. While these companies do well enough, not one can claim a defensible worldwide brand on the order of Sony, Levi's, Gillette, Wrigley, or Nike. Is the absence of a truly global brand in the nature of the products they offer, or might it be attributable to the local concessions they've made to their brands' integrity?

One Brand, One System

The power enjoyed by a worldwide brand is certainly reason enough to act globally, but there are even sweeter rewards. One benefit of aligned sourcing, central support systems, and consistent processes is that you eliminate unnecessary complexity. That means higher quality, lower costs, and fewer wasted resources. Another advantage is the ability to replicate best practices, such as training and market research programs, in all operations.

But as powerful as these advantages are, few companies seem willing to step up to a global challenge. This is partly a matter of conditioning. Some companies with secondary brands aren't in the habit of thinking of themselves as global contenders. Preferring the quick win, they go into smaller countries, resist taking the lead or dominating the category, and hope that, with their short-term profits, they can defend their position by the time an attacker arrives. It's a de facto defense not sustainable over the long haul.

Global players, on the other hand, actively look to win big markets even in the face of adversity. The first McDonald's stores in the Netherlands lost money for nearly a decade because the company's supply sources couldn't consistently deliver to the product's specified quality. Local managers clamored for local product. The bitter lessons McDonald's learned about the dangers of customizing against core positioning have been etched permanently in its memory. Today the company earns more than half its profit outside the U.S.

Taking the First Steps

We're not saying that small concessions to local tastes should never be made or that multinationals shouldn't learn from regionals—especially in Asian markets. The key is to tweak on the margin without affecting image, quality, processes, or cost. Levi's blue jeans may be cut differently for Mexico than they are for Minnesota, but store service and brand are consistent the world over. The metric system may necessitate calling a Quarter-Pounder a Royale in France, but the process, sourcing, and staff training still shout McDonald's loud and clear.

The next decade will be a telling one in international markets. Giving in to local pressures too quickly could forever hurt your chances for a truly global brand. Ask yourself:

- Have I established a specific program for market ranking, global brand development, quality control, and consumer targeting?

- Do my localization concessions cost more than they add? Do they make me less efficient? Do they compromise brand image or quality?

- Have I created common and clearly defined processes for new product rollout, market research, competitive reporting, sales support, and human resources tracking?

- Do I control the consumer's experience, and am I creating emotional engagement and repetition—in other words, consumer *wow*?

In the rush to go global, look before you leap. Most companies make some local concessions, but too many make more than necessary. The point is to have a well-reasoned, fact-based strategy for how much is appropriate in what circumstances and for how long. Understand the pitfalls and seize the real—not ephemeral—opportunities. Use your priority markets to build deep positions and sustainable infrastructure; institute consistent reporting, research, and human-resources-tracking systems; and hold ruthlessly to principles. Cut a path a mile deep, not a mile wide.

This article was first published in April 1997.

John Wong and Marcus Bökkerink

With an expanding economy, an increasing demand for consumer goods, and growing brand awareness, China is seen by most multinational companies as a prime opportunity. While this is true, the macro overview misses a minefield of local challenges that could make realizing China's promise harder than people think. The bottom line is that what it takes to succeed in China is rapidly changing.

Until recently, multinational consumer-goods companies could depend on superior brand-management skills, global technologies, and financial muscle to mount a successful product introduction and rollout. Now those advantages are accessible to growing numbers of international competitors and even to aggressive local survivors. Increasingly, they're just table stakes for getting into the game—which is also changing.

The battle for market dominance has progressed beyond the beachheads of Shanghai, Beijing, and a few other developed cities to the rest of urban—and even the wealthier parts of rural—China. That territory includes more than 600 urban centers—70 with more than a million people. Marketers will need new strategies to succeed in this diverse and expanding new frontier. We believe that intense focus on local implementation will be the key. To appreciate the importance of this shift in focus, you need to understand the nature of China's rapidly evolving markets.

Dynamic Fragmentation

Western multinational companies (MNCs) may think they understand marketing to diverse regions, but in most cases the challenges they've experienced pale before China's vast multiplicity. Not only do China's many markets differ greatly from one another, but each market is evolving in its own way. Examples of this "dynamic fragmentation" are regions that differ in the following ways:

- **Growth rates and incomes.** A product may be at the end of its life cycle in one market and at the beginning in another.

- **Needs and tastes.** In Guangzhou and Beijing, for example, different living conditions, eating habits, and media exposure result in different usage patterns.

- **Wholesale and retail trade channels.** In some cities, trade is consolidated; in others, it's fragmented. Discounters are emerging in the south, while department store cartels rule in many central cities. Some big-city department stores and distributors are expanding their wholesale business into outlying cities and towns, while in other cities local wholesalers are consolidating their hold on individual markets.

- **Competitive history.** In many categories, each region has its own favorite brands. These local survivors are formidable, unlike the local competitors the MNCs have succeeded in displacing during the first phase of consolidation. What's more, some of these strong local players are building on their regional strength to expand geographically.

Marketing to different regions, which are evolving at different rates and are served through different channels by different competitors, calls for attention to local detail at the most granular level, from sell-in to sell-through. But there's a second reason to focus on local implementation.

Old-World Infrastructure

China's trade and distribution channels are still unsophisticated, especially outside the most developed cities. High-quality transportation infrastructure is limited, regulations constrain third-party providers, and transit times and costs are unpredictable. Retailers with modern purchasing and payment practices are only just emerging. Meanwhile, most distributors—wholesalers in all but name—provide little added value.

As for the marketing infrastructure, macroeconomic and demographic data are sporadic and unreliable. Third-party research is available, but it has limited depth and reach and covers only some products. Television commercials are common, as are advertising agencies, but the media markets are highly localized. There are hundreds of provincial and local television stations, and more than a thousand local city and enterprise cable channels.

The combination of continuing regional fragmentation and old-world infrastructure makes local implementation essential and *superior* local implementation a powerful competitive advantage. The ability to customize not only products and formats but also brand positioning, trade programs, sell-in approaches, and sell-through tactics will outweigh older strategies that rely on advertising scale and standardized promotions. Even the MNCs with strong home markets won't be able to avoid those changes. But if they move quickly to develop local implementation capabilities in addition to their structural advantages, they will be hard to displace.

Best-Practice Examples

A few multinationals have already begun to do battle. In its initial rollout of skin soaps, for example, Procter & Gamble complemented its traditional broad-scale advertising with individual samplings and some customizing in fragrance and feel. To compensate for the lack of infrastructure and to ensure consistent coverage and inventory while testing different promotions, it trains and deploys a large force of foot-soldier students, local sales teams, stockists, and sales managers in primary and secondary cities.

Some overseas Chinese competitors are playing the same game, notwithstanding their lack of P&G-level resources. Ting Yi and Want Want, two Taiwanese food companies, have handily beaten MNCs in share, growth, and profits in broad food categories. Like leading MNCs, they've tailored their products to local tastes and built strong brand recognition in the market. But unlike most MNCs, they overcame a poor trade infrastructure by manufacturing in multiple cities, working with more than 1,000 wholesalers to manage their inventories and local deliveries, and distributing directly to more than 2,000 retailers with a fleet of more than 200 trucks. As a result, they enjoy five to ten times the geographic coverage and three to four times the channel penetration of a typical MNC.

Some domestic companies have also refined their local implementation skills while developing world-class technology, scale in advertising, and investment in brand marketing that match multinational levels. They are overcoming their Chinese competitors with these structural advantages and beating back the MNCs with the combination of structural and local advantages.

The appliance company Haier, for example, has built the strongest service and direct sell-though network in China and outmaneuvered its rivals with city-specific promotion campaigns. It enjoys a higher market share and price premium in refrigerators than joint venture products from MNCs such as Bosch-Siemens, Samsung, and Whirlpool—and it has started to replicate this success in washing machines.

Meeting the Challenge

How do you build the infrastructure and capabilities for superior local implementation? The first step is to understand that you can't do it overnight. Nor will investing a lot of money necessarily make it happen faster.

But you *will* have to invest in human resources, especially in the early years and at the level most companies reserve for plant and brand initiatives. And you'll need to be closely involved in all activities that make up the brand-management value chain.

Here are some of the actions that the best-practice companies we've worked with recommend:

Consumer Insight. Successful marketers supplement third-party research with in-house resources and students to canvass competitors, retailers, and consumers in individual city markets. They also invest in MIS systems and train their sales force and merchandisers to deliver the information needed. The growth of a consumer knowledge base creates the opportunity map.

Demand Development. To reinforce advertising in China's new markets, best-practice marketers emphasize such below-the-line activities as:

- **In-store retailing.** Marketers develop retail capabilities with in-store sell-through personnel. Domestic competitors in particular have brought micromarketing into the store with their own "retail" infrastructure of several hundred in-store promoters and merchandisers.

- **Experimentation.** Marketers deploy different promotion programs in different cities and stores to learn which ones work best and where. Then they customize to local market conditions.

- **Decentralization.** Marketers delegate significant authority over local promotion budgets, print advertising, and even pricing to regional sales managers in order to encourage responsiveness and local sell-in and sell-through integration. While they don't avoid mistakes with this practice (local resources are woefully undertrained), they beat their competitors at establishing a presence. In addition, they discover their own future highfliers along the way.

Sell-In. Best-practice marketers invest in distributor infrastructure, assigning full-time personnel to compensate for unskilled distributors and providing their own temporary foot soldiers to penetrate a region completely. And they're not afraid to overinvest in direct sales. Although the salaries of good salespeople are rising in China, local economics justify direct selling to department stores at lower sales volumes than in the West. Best-practice competitors are expanding the role of their frontline salespeople beyond sell-in, customer relationships, and collection to integrated sell-through and micromarketing.

Operations Platform. Successful MNCs go to market with broad product portfolios. Brand awareness in China is created by a full display of products in the store, especially outside major cities. In fast-moving consumables as well as durables, smart players leverage a limited number of product platforms or technologies to introduce a broad range of product SKUs. These products may reduce near-term margins because of higher-cost manufacturing or logistics, but they deliver an early trade presence and help marketers discover the hard-to-predict bestsellers.

The Local Advantage

China's expanding frontier has put local implementation at the top of the strategy agenda. And because this plays to the strengths of domestic rather than multinational players, it is forcing many consumer goods MNCs to rethink their business model in China. Brand management and product technology will remain as essential as ever, but without superior implementation at the local level, these capabilities will be ineffective, undifferentiated, and merely incremental.

Superior local advantage will take time to build and require considerable investment in money and human resources, but once achieved, it will be very difficult to replicate, even for competitors with deep pockets. Not surprisingly, companies that lead in this advantage are achieving immediate tactical wins in the field as well as acquiring longer-term structural advantages in brand dominance and scale.

This article was first published in July 1997.

Marcus Bökkerink and Wahid Hamid

 By now, most multinational consumer companies have arrived in Asia. Growth has come easily for many, but sustained profits remain elusive. As more competitors enter the field, traditional entry strategies are being replaced with ambitious plans aimed at delivering both profitable growth and sustainable competitive positions as quickly as possible. Eager as the local management teams are, however, their organizations lack the depth and experience of their companies back home. Asia's unique environment only accentuates those deficiencies. The result is a frustrating gap between what multinational companies (MNCs) want to achieve in Asia and what their organizations can actually deliver.

To avoid settling for less, MNCs must take a different approach in Asia. They must decentralize some areas while centralizing others, and they must be flexible enough to tailor different solutions for different country markets, and even for different activities within the same function. The trick is getting the balance right.

The Case for Decentralization

The Asian market is unlike other markets in at least three ways. First, although already significant as a region, it is actually a collection of highly fragmented and diverse markets, each with distinct consumer needs, trade structures, and competitors.

Second, compared with mature and concentrated markets in the West, Asian markets are rapidly changing. Even Japan's mature market has been markedly altered by the emergence of modern formats, especially discounters. One result is that aggressive MNCs and local companies have improved their positions by tailoring their offerings to take advantage of these new streamlined distribution channels.

Third, because of incremental expansion and differing local regulations, most multinationals have accumulated a diverse portfolio of large and small subsidiaries, joint ventures, and offices—each with its own business purpose, cost structure, and organizational issues.

These characteristics have driven many consumer goods companies to emphasize speed, local responsiveness, and market differentiation, which call for a highly decentralized organization and entrepreneurial, local decision-making. Reinforcing this approach is the fact that many multinationals' Asian operations are not only institutionally young and eclectic but also located far from the parent's core markets and the corporate center.

The problem, however, is that across-the-board decentralization in Asia is difficult to achieve in practice and often inappropriate.

The Forces Against Decentralization

As logical as a decentralized approach to Asia's markets might seem, several factors argue against it. First, there's an acute shortage of middle and senior managers capable of making effective decisions in individual markets; and qualified expatriate and local managers, when available, command exceptionally high salaries.

Second, while some Asian markets are large enough to benefit from decentralization, others are too small and unprofitable to warrant it.

Third, the costs of using different practices throughout Asia can be high. Divergent product policies, for example, can create complexities that negate scale economies. Companies with regional or global brands need to ensure that the effect of portfolio, positioning, and even marketing and pricing decisions in different markets doesn't undermine the profitability of the region as a whole.

Fourth, in some markets—such as China, Japan, and Korea—high-level strategy, capital investment, and brand decisions require the active collaboration and involvement of senior officers at the center.

Such factors have driven some MNCs to centralize management and functions across markets and geographies, and to encourage regional coordination. For many, however, this integration has resulted in an organization that lacks responsiveness, creates bureaucracy, and becomes a justification for large regional centers.

Compromising Positions

For consumer goods companies in particular, Asia's situation magnifies the perennial organizational conflicts between centralization and decentralization, and between integrating activities across markets and duplicating them within markets.

One central-leaning organization, for instance, controlled strategy development, planning, budgeting, and product development by centralizing all product, positioning, and marketing decisions in the Asian and corporate headquarters. Organizationally, this meant a functional reporting structure duplicated in each country. The approach was costly, however, and it generated endless conflicts between local organizations and corporate headquarters. As a result, the company missed market opportunities.

A highly decentralized company, on the other hand, suffered a significant slowdown in growth after an initial period of rapid success because of its inability to roll out product adaptation and brand skills across the region. Successful businesses in Thailand and Japan were joined by struggling operations in China and Indonesia. Entrepreneurial dealmaking, critical for success on initial entry, led to uncoordinated decisions, duplicated support functions, and different systems across markets, adding to already high costs. Moreover, the best people were not in charge of the most important markets, and the best in-country talent was focused more on administering fully functional operations than on developing demand.

Another decentralized company left the positioning and pricing of one of its global flagship brands to local management in Korea. Lacking the capabilities to stand up to new competition, the local team lowered the price of the global brand to protect share, destroying brand image and profitability. Now the damage is almost irreversible.

Such compromised positions are particularly difficult to unwind in Asia. For the companies cited above, the combination of different cultural norms, scarcity of local talent, and other restrictions significantly slowed their ability to restructure the organization and redeploy people.

Finding the Right Balance

The way out of the centralization/decentralization dilemma is to combine the best elements of both. Traditional broad-brush approaches need to be replaced by more precise tailoring and "de-averaging" of the organizational solution by market, decision process, and activity, even within the same function. Companies need to maintain the benefits of local initiative where it is most appropriate, while sharing experience and expertise across markets. That means redefining structures and roles—not only for country organizations but also for the Asian and corporate centers that manage them.

Studies by The Boston Consulting Group have shown that the most successful organizations in Asia use the following broad principles when tailoring their organizations in this way:

- Design separate organizational solutions for strategic and tactical decision-making, especially when it comes to product investments and marketing.

- Resist the temptation to overstretch your best people. Focus the most capable managers on demand development and sales execution, not on "general" management administration. Have them work out of large strategic markets and report directly to the Asian regional president or senior global officers.

- Centralize decisions for smaller markets within lead markets, and outsource noncritical activities to focused players.

- Consolidate responsibility for in-country support functions, such as human resources, finance, and manufacturing, at the highest possible level. This will reinforce in-country managers' focus on critical strategy, marketing, and commercial decisions. It will also strengthen the center's ability to monitor performance and manage the placement of key talent across the region.

- Elevate the importance of human resources management—recruiting, training, and career development—to maximize existing potential and increase the loyalty of local talent.

- Make sure that capabilities requirements and compensation reflect the different responsibilities faced by managers in nominally similar positions but in different markets.

Managing the Balance

Multinational companies need to evaluate markets, functions, and specific activities according to their suitability for a particular approach and then choose which activities to decentralize and centralize. They need to distinguish critical markets from important but noncritical markets, and in some cases to adjust their goals to the available talent and anticipated economics.

The tensions between centralization and decentralization, however, may never be entirely reconciled, and the risk that one side will be compromised is ever present. The most effective organizations develop specific integrating mechanisms that directly address these risks and improve the quality of decisions made within the Asian organizations. The following are a few of them:

- To ensure compatible decentralized decisions, they make sure that local decision-makers and senior managers share beliefs on strategic priorities, how the business works, what drives advantage, and how to generate value.

- For effective centralized decisions, they make sure the right local information is captured by using guidance templates or local (rather than regional) surveys, or by requiring daily communication between the central brand manager and in-country people.

- To increase cross-country experience sharing, they establish formal brand-management and sales task forces.

- To encourage bottom-up integration, they assign regional responsibility for specific products to specific countries or identify best-country resources to roll out a centrally defined competency.

Managing the Organization's Evolution

Making sure that the Asian organization uses the right structure and mechanisms requires a rigorous process.

---

1. Set the context by developing an understanding of
- global/Asia vision and strategy
- business economics
- critical versus other markets
- ongoing internal initiatives

2. Develop a structural blueprint by
- dividing functions into key decisions and support activities
- identifying dominant drivers and constraints to centralization and decentralization
- developing a "clean sheet" view of each decision process and responsibility by function and market

3. Evaluate the status quo, including
- current decision processes and responsibilities
- where they diverge from actual practice—and from the "clean sheet" view

4. Determine how to manage the compromise by
- ensuring the compatibility of decentralized decisions
- enhancing the specificity of centralized decisions
- reinforcing the capabilities of local resources
- simplifying the approach in smaller markets
- promoting value-added from the center

5. Develop a game plan to manage the evolution by
- prioritizing a reorganization of markets, functions, and activities
- developing a human resources plan that includes local and expatriate resources
- adopting detailed policies, systems, and mechanisms to make the evolution possible

Companies that allow their organizations to evolve gradually in Asia risk ending up with intractable problems that take years to remedy. No single model will work for every company, but under the leadership of an activist center, each company can design the best organizational solution for its specific situation—one that meets its compromises head-on before they destroy the potential for profitable growth in Asia.

This article was first published in November 1997.

Wahid Hamid and Dave Young

The economic crisis in East Asia is presenting multinational retailers and consumer goods companies with a rare opportunity to retain current cus-  tomers, attract new ones, and reshape their industries. But it won't be easy. Companies already in Asia face the challenge of realigning their current businesses with new realities. And new entrants need to understand rapidly changing economies. Both must act quickly to take advantage of the considerable shifts in consumer markets, distribution channels, commercial relationships, and competitive landscapes.

Consumer Markets

Multinational companies (MNCs) without established brand loyalties in East Asia will need to rethink product portfolios, pricing, and positioning. From Jakarta to Seoul, people are consuming less, switching to lower-priced products, searching out promotions, and shopping at cheaper stores. Department store sales are down more than 40 percent, demand for luxury goods is down nearly 60 percent, and "fashionable" people no longer line up to get into new restaurants and bistros. But discount retail sales are increasing, traditional products are enjoying a comeback, and affordable entertainment is flourishing.

Companies shouldn't jump to the conclusion that this is an across-the-board downscaling, however. A leading MNC in Korea made that mistake when it assumed that its customers would switch from the company's premium products to its lower-priced offerings. Hoping to increase volume to make up for lower prices, the company refocused sales, advertising, and promotion spending onto the less expensive products. But the actual response was more complicated. Premium-price customers cut down on frequency and amount but did not trade down. Low-price customers defected to even lower-priced Korean substitutes. The resulting demand was heavily skewed toward the premium categories, and overall volume declined.

MNCs must understand—down to the subtlest detail—how *their* customers are responding to the economic depression. Are they buying less, and less frequently? How much are they willing to spend and for what occasions? Furthermore, MNCs must understand how each consumer segment is responding to each of their categories, adjacent categories, and brands.

That level of knowledge will help them answer such strategic questions as:

- How much of our current demand is short-term? Can we influence this demand? Can we win lost customers back?

- Do we have the right products in our current portfolio? Where are the gaps and how can we fill them?

- How should our marketing program change? How much should we spend and how should we position our products?

- What kind of demand can we expect for current and potential products after the crisis?

MNCs must also consider the reaction against foreign brands. This is particularly strong in Korea, where consumers are switching to local products in an effort to keep jobs at home. Even some locally manufactured foreign brands are perceived to be taking wealth out of the region—a situation that has prompted those companies to advertise their contribution to the local economy and its export competitiveness. The nationalist sentiment could fade over time, but MNCs must confront it today.

To fight a nationalist backlash, MNCs with mostly global brands might customize their global campaigns to resonate with local interests and might work with government agencies, wholesaler associations, and community organizations to build goodwill. MNCs could also fight the backlash from within stores. As thousands of local manufacturers go bankrupt every month and survivors have trouble maintaining full production, MNCs can use their financial power to keep their products on the shelves.

Finally, MNCs could acquire local companies with strong domestic brands to shield them from nationalist sentiment or to capture customers as they go domestic. They'll need to move quickly—some of the best local enterprises have already been the targets of foreign buyers—but not so quickly that they don't screen potential companies carefully for actual profitability, hidden liabilities, human resources issues, and employees' resentment of foreign ownership.

Distribution Channels

As one local distributor after another succumbs to the crisis, consumer goods and retail companies alike must deal with dissolving relationships in their local channels. Even the distributors that survive the crisis may not be able to track consumers as they shift to new segments.

The fact that many once-powerful local distributors are now in trouble isn't all bad, however, because it offers multinationals the opportunity to exploit these power shifts in order to create a more efficient distribution system. Moving from today's messy reality to an orderly system will be tricky, however. It will involve evaluating current distributors' accountability, business practices, and profit margins, and helping the best ones survive. By working with other MNCs, companies can lend financial support to the distributors with the healthiest business practices and can thereby gain control over this strategic part of the value chain.

In addition to strategies for dealing with distributors, some consumer goods MNCs are focusing on the retailing landscape, in such areas as:

- **Key accounts.** As some retailers go bankrupt, others—mostly large foreign discounters such as Wal-Mart and Carrefour—are investing aggressively in the region.

- **Receivables.** MNCs are assessing those debtors at risk and tightening credit policies to minimize further exposure. At the same time, they are striving to maintain sales volume—a tough tradeoff because exposure can be greatest with high-volume distributors.

Commercial Relationships

Given the devaluating currencies, collapsing prices, falling demand, low liquidity, and easing of local regulatory requirements throughout East Asia, MNCs have an enormous opportunity to acquire local manufacturers and, perhaps more important, to restructure their current joint ventures and partnerships.

Several consumer goods MNCs are already offering attractive cash infusions to desperate local manufacturers and current partners in exchange for an entry position, higher equity, more management control, or the rights to a strong local brand. These companies should realize, however, that reaping the payoffs from their investments could take considerable time and management attention. Before structuring such deals, MNCs need to consider the following questions:

- How will the local industry and consumers react to foreign ownership?

- How hard will it be to attract talented managers?

- Should downsizing be part of the initial deal, considering that workers' reactions to layoffs by foreign acquirers could be very negative?

- Do we need access to the selling company's distribution arrangements, support services, and government relations?

- Can we ensure that the selling company has a stake in the new company, perhaps by arranging a board membership for one or two of the previous owners?

Competitive Landscapes

The economic crisis in East Asia is creating new winners and losers. MNCs need to develop game plans for the various scenarios that could occur. To avoid being blind-sided, they should ask themselves the following questions:

- Could our competitors destroy our current advantage by acquiring a local company and catapulting to a higher share position?

- Could new or existing competitors strike deals with our current partners, creating a conflict of interest or diminishing the value of existing relationships?

- Are local players behaving rationally during the downturn, given the need to dress up for a potential sale? What should our response be?

The Asian economy will rebound. Creating a position of strength will never be less expensive than it is today. Before the economy bounces back, MNCs should nail down a profitable future in East Asia.

This article was first published in September 1998.

Part Eight

STAYING AHEAD

Jacques Chapuis

Athletes know they can't win unless they believe they can win. Business leaders are no different. In a recent survey, CEOs of leading consumer-goods and retail companies all cited growth as a top priority. But they also listed plenty of obstacles: a sluggish economy, mature markets, decreasing differentiation, pressure on margins, rising costs. Are these concerns outweighing their belief in growth?

It would seem so. Many consumer and retail companies have been shelving plans for expansion, focusing instead on rationalization, restructuring, downsizing, and divestitures. But companies that have abandoned their faith in growth may be mistaken on at least two counts.

First, they seem to have forgotten that growth is an imperative at all times for all businesses in all sectors. Growth pulls in investors, reinforces competitive positioning, attracts and retains the best employees (by giving them greater, more rewarding opportunities), and energizes the organization. What's more, these elements are exactly the ones required to generate growth. Growth is the engine of a virtuous circle, a perpetual motion machine whose fuel is belief in growth.

Second, some companies mistakenly assume that growth opportunities are determined primarily by external factors: the market, competitors, technology, and so on. Yet companies as varied as PepsiCo, British Airways, Home Depot, and L'Oréal have managed to sustain consistent growth during economic downturns and in fiercely competitive industries. Growth is always possible when senior managers believe in it and when they instill that belief in the organization.

Gillette: Limited by Its Beliefs

Consider the example of Gillette. From the early 1970s to the mid-1980s, its share of the shaving-products market hovered at around 50 percent—a steady grip on what seemed to be a mature, no-growth, or certainly slow-growth, market. Then, between 1988 and 1993, Gillette's market share soared to 65 percent. Suddenly, it seemed, the company had completely revamped its brand with a new product and a new communication strategy. Gillette had launched the highly innovative Sensor razors in a stunningly successful worldwide rollout.

Gillette found growth the old-fashioned way: by investing in its core brand. Why had it languished so long before doing so? The short answer is that Gillette's unexamined beliefs about growth had obstructed its vision. But those beliefs were grounded in a difficult-to-dislodge history, as beliefs often are.

In the 1980s in the U.S., disposable razors were thought to be the wave of the future. Initially resisting this trend, Gillette eventually felt compelled to offer its own disposable products. Overseas, growth opportunities for the company's traditional shaving systems were rejected on the assumption that emerging international markets were not interested in premium products. Gillette had accepted the inevitability of low margins and growth, settling into what it thought was a mature market.

Fortunately, as it turns out, the financial markets had other ideas. In three consecutive years beginning in 1986, Gillette was attacked by raiders. That proved to be the wake-up call. With the Sensor razor, Gillette challenged its conviction that it couldn't increase market share with a higher-priced, better product. Even more telling is that the technology for the Sensor had been in development since the late 1970s, but, doubting the potential for growth, Gillette had been unwilling to risk bringing the product forward.

Looking for Growth Opportunities

All companies harbor beliefs about their markets, and the more successful the company, the stronger its beliefs. This is natural and good, as long as the beliefs are tested regularly against new perspectives and creative possibilities. One way of testing convictions about growth is to rediscover the consumer. Consumers buy; "markets" do not. Markets often are fictions that disguise real consumers and their wants and needs. Understanding when and why consumers buy or fail to buy will always reveal new growth opportunities. Therefore:

- **Take a broader view of your market.** What groups buy too few of your products and why? When Gillette finally understood women's shaving needs, it invested in designing a razor specifically for women. Women stopped using disposables and made the Sensor for Women their product of choice.

- **Expand your relationship with consumers.** Why do consumers stop using your product? Understanding that toddlers are not toilet trained overnight, Kimberly-Clark developed Huggies Pull-Ups, extending the period during which diapers are worn.

- **Break compromises imposed on consumers.** What tradeoffs are your customers forced to make when buying your products? Until Chrysler offered the minivan, families shopping for a car were forced to choose a sedan, a station wagon, or a truck.

The CEO's Attitude Matters

Persuading an organization to believe in endless possibilities for growth is the leader's responsibility. It is not automatic. He or she will need to maintain direct and continuous contact with consumers, sensing in a personal way the desires and frustrations of buyers and signaling to the organization that time with customers matters. He or she will need to create an environment in which people feel comfortable challenging established beliefs. Leaders of growth companies encourage risk taking and discourage "It can't be done."

Wayne Calloway, former chairman and CEO of PepsiCo, presided over a company with a strong growth record—a consequence of his own strong conviction:

> Growth is pure oxygen. It creates a vital, enthusiastic corporation where people see genuine personal opportunity. They take bigger chances. They work harder and smarter. In that way growth is more than our single most important financial driver: it's an essential part of our corporate culture. (PepsiCo Annual Report, 1995)

Winning companies, like winning athletes, know that conviction beats the odds every time.

This article was first published in July 1996.

Barry Jones and Michael J. Silverstein

Management dogma can stifle breakthrough insight. Companies lose their edge trying to hold on to the status quo or, worse, to yesterday's reasons for winning. The more triumphant a company is, the tougher the challenge to see the need for change and fast response. It is the paradox of success.

Sometimes a start-up company's advantage is its very lack of history. Mature competitors often use past success as a shield against new ideas. Consensus and conflict avoidance impede a quick response to threats.

The hair on the back of your neck should stand up when you hear any variation of "This new opportunity will never be as profitable as our base business" or "Don't worry—that start-up is growing fast but it's losing money."

To catch competitors off guard, you must often be introspective and contrary, and always *curious, intuitive,* and *bold.* Driving a successful business to new success and new arenas requires a taste for challenge, an acceptance of confrontation, and a willingness to break the rules. It also calls for a continuous infusion of new market facts, a healthy dose of skepticism, and a commitment to resolving consumer dissatisfactions.

Here, for the New Year, are seven observations about success.

1. Organizations naturally slip to the mean.

Accomplishment breeds complacency. Some degree of angst is necessary to maintain an edge. The worst losses are often the result of failure to drive to domination after an early win. Frequently, the difference between almost reaching a stretch goal and getting there is boldness backed by rigorous analysis and execution. Advantage is a combination of courage and applied knowledge.

2. Consensus and mediocrity can go hand in hand.

The drive to get along can inhibit breakthrough solutions. Day-to-day pressures often lead to the path of least resistance while new competitive arenas are lost. Don't let the desire for organizational consensus stand in the way of new business models. Seek out the contrary opinion and the fresh perspective. Get small breakthrough teams to surface, test, and pursue creative new ideas.

3. *Process* can be a seductive word.

Many managers who have lost their nerve hide behind a self-serving defini-tion of process. This can be a pretext for inaction and an energy-sapping form of democracy. Processes that result in speed, common frameworks, and commitment can be a source of global advantage. But process for its own sake can become a crutch, an excuse, and an empty exercise. Good process leaders often tilt in favor of the contrary view if it is supported by the facts.

4. Invest when you're ahead.

The extended development time of new ideas and their uncertain payback are luxuries few businesses can afford. Yet if there is one time they can afford them, it is when things are going well. At the moment of peak performance, opportunities abound. Seize the advantage by investing in proprietary tech-nology, advanced consumer knowledge, and retail intelligence. Drive the business for further advantage.

5. Failure can create paralysis.

Winning is a matter of experience, of persistence, of practice. Many com-panies are paralyzed by failure, retreat at early defeat, and then dismiss ini-tiative with the refrain "We've tried that before." The lessons from failure can open a new path to success. The greater the access to the market, the greater the opportunities for experimentation. The best teacher is the fail-ure to satisfy every aspect of the consumer's needs.

6. Humans are not created equal in every dimension.

Equality can be a harmful fiction. People advance at different rates, in dif-ferent ways, for different goals. Creativity and inspiration are not evenly apportioned. Anxiety, drive, energy, and superior knowledge are the strongest determinants of success. Recognize your own strengths and weak-nesses: your intuitive skills or your tendency to ignore opposing ideas. Com-plement your leadership with breakthrough teams to put hard facts or creativity on the table.

7. Trust your instincts.

Organizations fear change. They have a high tolerance for sloth and the status quo. That's why you have to concentrate your forces for victory. Orga-nizations rarely create blinding strategy. But leaders and small breakthrough teams can. Be bold—create the fortune of tomorrow.

It is no accident that most New Year's resolutions fade quickly. The pressures from day to day and from quarter to quarter are relentless. However, if you use your resolutions to pause, regain your breath and your energies, refresh, and renew, then once again you will maintain the attacker's advantages.

This article was first published in January 1997.

Barry Jones and Michael J. Silverstein

"I wish the leaders of our businesses were experts. I wish they had intimate knowledge of our consumers. I wish I could say we are building a platform of knowledge—intricate, complete, and easy to tap,"  laments the CEO of a leading global packaged-goods company. He and many others are focused on what is becoming the question of the day: How do we create organizations whose insights into the hopes and dreams of consumers give them total command of their markets?

Domain expertise—superior knowledge of and insight into a business or category—leads to greater creativity, more innovation, more movement, and more excitement in the market. It requires teams that have been in the domain long enough to have learned all there is to know about it and to have added to the circle of knowledge; and it requires the expertise to be embedded in the organization, in its culture, and in "the way we do things around here."

Like Pablo Picasso, who began his prolific career by studying classical painting, managers must understand the basics before they can innovate beyond them. Picasso first learned line drawing, reproductive portraiture, and the use of light and color before he began innovating with those skills. He mastered shapes and quality of line, which he later transmuted and recombined into new forms.

Picasso's creative migration from classical technical excellence to a holistic reconception of form, space, and time resulted from domain expertise. His skill as a draftsman permitted new stylization of the human figure. Concentration and experience led to breakthrough. He condensed a lifetime of conventional drawing and painting in the decade before his twenty-first birthday. Because he had complete command of his artistic domain, he could go on to create cubism and his own version of surrealism.

In business, Gillette is the Picasso of razor blades. In the past decade, this shaving-domain expert first introduced Atra Plus, with a pivoting head and lubricating strip, then the Sensor blade, which adjusts to your face for "the best shave a man can get," and finally Sensor Excel, with microfibers that stretch the skin for an even closer shave. In a year or so, Gillette plans to launch the next generation of razors in 70 countries around the globe. Each innovation has added value for the consumer and commanded a higher price. That has translated into $40 billion in market value. Category focus

and consumer knowledge—domain expertise leading to domain dominance—have been the drivers of this success story.

Domain experts are single-minded about their areas. They intimately
understand their customers and their behavior. They understand consumption patterns and drivers, consumer tradeoffs, inventory patterns, performance expectations, disappointments, compromises in delivery, and
product availability. Seasoned experts use this insight to spur innovation, to
see through complexities, and to imagine what could be. Their knowledge
is an opportunity for change, not a grip on the status quo.

Characteristics of Domain Experts

Domain experts see patterns of order and change. They aren't caught flat-
footed by a market shift or a new competitor. Because they are in the marketplace, eye to eye and nose to nose with their customers, they can be
moving before the market has twitched.

Domain experts are both introspective and retrospective. They ask why
the category or business works the way it does. They review competitor activity and draw incisive lessons from their own and their competitors' victories
and losses. In their view, a loss is an opportunity for refinement and success.

Domain experts take their insights from patterns of consumer activity.
Rather than delegate consumer research, they put themselves next to the
consumer by going to the places where consumers shop and even into their
homes. What's more, discussions with consumers extend from first-order
concerns to latent needs that go beyond incremental improvement efforts.
This is the material that permits leaps, not creeps. True domain experts bring
both facts and emotion to understanding consumers' needs. Their direct
observations lead to creative new ways to use a product and to dramatic
improvements in its performance. They see every consumer contact, every
failure to surpass expectations, as an opportunity to learn. They broaden
the definition of the domain.

Ely Callaway, founder of Callaway Golf, knew before he created Big
Bertha that every golfer dreams of the perfect swing and the sweet kiss of
contact with the ball. He knew that a larger "sweet spot" would provide a
firmer feel, more consistent yardage, easier hitting, and greater stability. His
intuition told him that the reaction to a truly innovative product from a fragmented and unsatisfied golf-equipment market would be, "I must have one."
Callaway went on to augment his innovation with line extensions, geographic
expansion, technology investments, and marketing savvy. "Develop a product that's demonstrably superior and pleasingly different, and then mer-

chandise the hell out of it," he says. He also understood that a golfer's biggest game is played on the fairway of the mind.

Callaway created domain expertise. As owner and manager of Callaway Golf for more than a decade, he also created more than $2 billion in value. With its understanding of golfers' psychology, physics, and human biomechanics, the Callaway Golf organization lives and breathes golf innovation.

Domain experts think with both sides of their brain. They use logic (facts and a quantitative understanding of activity) *and* intuition (crystallizing insight into what could be). You never hear domain experts dismiss an idea because it has been tried and failed. Most important, domain experts are curious and independent. They force uncompromising straight communication. Their "break the business" insights come from daily sweat, not a one-time event. Domain experts know that to stay ahead they must extend the boundaries—starting today and continuing tomorrow.

Because companies often become trapped within their own logic, the seed corn for starting a coterie of domain experts may need to come from outside the company. In addition, creating an organization where domain expertise is the rule, not the exception, requires:

- **Immersion in domain.** Advance from thinking about job rotation or time in grade to immersion in domain. Many multinationals move their best talent around in a mode of two-year job rotation. Others are trying to slow this down but are still focusing on a variety of experiences in terms of functions, categories, and geographies. Domain experts retain their best staff within the domain, moving them up grades or across interdependent functions but continuing to deepen their insight into behavior within the domain.

- **A domain culture.** Establish a customized framework or platform for how the domain works, how consumers behave in pursuit of their aspirations, how they make tradeoffs between competitive offerings, and how they shop the aisle. Embed this understanding in the organization and require employees to continue to improve the platform and expand the art of the possible in the business.

- **Teamed discovery.** Establish a formal process for learning the knowledge base with exercises and exploration. Cross-functional teams discover the consumer together with in-depth consumer research. Each team member is schooled in the basics of the business and encouraged to contribute new knowledge.

- **Leadership.** Lead from in front, not from behind. Make sure the category team reflects the knowledge and beliefs of the senior manager. True expertise in the business should be reflected up and down the organization. The leader must set the pace and the vision.

- **One-to-one persistence.** Innovation requires breaking the rules, staying close to the customer, and taking risks. Often, first efforts fail or deliver below expectations. In the after-failure review, pick up the pieces, modify the execution, and deliver the value in the next wave. The team should find out what went wrong the first time and go for a second or even a third try. At Sony, for example, promotions are based on a manager's ability to capture learning from failure.

Domain expertise separates the dabbler from the pro. Established as the norm in a company, it raises the stakes for competitors and results in rapid share gain, category redefinition, customer loyalty, and value. It will also change the company's culture, producing a single-mindedness of purpose. If you aim for success over the long term, the cheap tricks for short-term burst go away.

To achieve domain expertise, the ping-pong of career management must slow to permit real contribution and a legacy of fundamental insight and accomplishment. Here are four sets of questions to ponder:

- Have you created domain expertise? Do you know what you don't know? Do you know what you think you know but may not be true?

- Are you laying the platform for a renaissance in your business based on original, pioneering consumer insight? Is "close to the customer" more than rhetoric?

- Are you providing for your inheritors in the next wave of growth? Will the legacy you leave be a richer tapestry of understanding and insight into customer compromises and latent dissatisfactions?

- Are you fully mining the biggest, most powerful, and most threatening ideas for revitalization? Can you describe the shift in your market that presents both opportunity and threat?

Not many of you will truthfully answer yes to all these questions. But you could. You could leave behind a legacy of power, insight, curiosity, and discovery. You could become a domain expert.

This article was first published in December 1997.

SEEDS OF DESTRUCTION

Michael J. Silverstein and Emmanuel Huet

Like most civilizations, companies typically progress from rapid growth to maturity and then begin a long and often painful decline. But is the decline inevitable? Can successful companies overcome complacency, competitive threats, and shifting markets?

Consumer companies are particularly vulnerable to rapid change. Ten of the 25 retailers that were the world's largest in 1960 have disappeared. Eight of the 25 retailers at the top in 1997 either didn't exist in 1960 or had nominal sales. Seven of the 25 consumer goods manufacturers with the highest revenues in 1960 no longer survive as independent entities. (See Exhibits 19 to 22.) The reality of consumer marketing is "innovate or die."

Change can overwhelm even the most capable management teams. Usually, change is forced on a company by consumers or competitors. It can occur when demand shifts (through new buying or usage patterns, or new consumer needs) or when a competitor approaches the market from a different vantage point, bringing new resources or a better response to a consumer problem. Many of the companies that succumbed in the last 40 years failed to respond to intruders. Others lost contact with consumers' shifting tastes. Focusing narrowly on their core businesses, they were blind to threats and opportunities beyond their limited vision. Eventually, they lost the ambition and creativity that had fueled their initial success.

Failing from Within

The forces that drive change may come from the outside, but a company's inability to respond to them is an internal disease that metastasizes quickly. Resources—human and otherwise—begin to flow out of the company as profits are dissipated, new investments earn below the hurdle rate, and advantage is squandered. Many companies sow the seeds of their own destruction in their initial success. The breakthrough innovation that originally opened new markets can also establish a model for success that shuts out fresh perspectives. Instead of inventing a new model, the company continues to follow the old one. Rigor mortis sets in.

Large companies are constantly in danger of becoming dinosaurs. Although their size gives them many advantages, it can also lead to some potentially devastating disadvantages, including

- increasing complexity costs, resulting in inflexibility and slow decision-making

- a tendency toward internal conflict and stratification

- a leadership that emphasizes capital investments as a solution to all problems

- centralized control with limited coordination among divisions and a weakened sense of market trends and dissatisfactions

It's easy for a consumer company to become a lumbering colossus, incapable of competing against leaner, faster, and more spirited businesses. But retailers face the greatest challenge. Many owe their success—and their customers' continued allegiance—to their founder's vision and their large investment in stores and systems. But when customers age, relocate, or demand new products, no one is able to convince the organization that it has to adapt or it will die.

The seeds of destruction are often visible to a discerning leader. The head of a multibillion-dollar consumer company recently lamented, "We've gained five share points in the last five years and achieved record earnings in 1997. But something happened this year. Volume is flat or declining. Competitors we had put out to pasture have come back with a vengeance. My old tricks—merchandising, cost control, rallying the troops—don't work anymore."

The CEO's company has grown dramatically, but so have its problems: Overhead is increasing at an alarming rate. Investments in IT have failed to deliver better decisions or an integrated information system. Key-account programs require six levels of approval and eight weeks of consideration before final sign-off. And the routine battles between marketing and sales are growing more heated. Efforts to break into new markets have failed, and the research department (renamed Consumer Insight) can't account for the shifts in demand. Yet because the business continues to show significant profits, it's all but impossible to get anyone to face up to the coming crisis and the company's need to reinvent itself.

The company has lost touch with consumers largely because it has allowed retailers to do the work of interpreting consumers' needs. Meanwhile, managers expend so much energy navigating the company's organizational structure that no one notices when a competitor runs away with an emerging market segment. The company needs to refocus on the world outside its walls. It needs to turn mounds of raw data on competitors into information it can act on; it needs to get much closer to consumers; and it needs to inspire its people to turn their swords on competitors instead of on each other. Companies that always reinvent themselves challenge their assumptions about market definition, sustainable cost position, changes in consumption, and the potential for competitive ambush.

Focusing Outward

Overcoming these destructive tendencies takes effort, vision, and commitment. For a company to succeed, it must adapt to new realities without discarding the wisdom it has acquired through experience. It must respond to intruders while seeding the organization with the intellectual diversity and vitality necessary for its continuing evolution. But the real key to this work is in the millions of details that begin to form a picture of consumers' and competitors' movements. If you suspect your company could find itself in the same spot as the one described above, consider these questions:

- Have you shopped along with consumers lately? Can you describe their experience from purchase to repurchase? What are their biggest dissatisfactions? Do you know when and why they defect?

- Have you tried to understand your competitors' consumers with the same intensity as you have your own? Do you have data on how often they buy your products and on their intentions to repurchase?

- Do you know your competitors' bestsellers? Do you track competitors' test markets and adapt or improve on profitable ideas at the earliest sign of success?

- Do you measure the efficiency of your marketing efforts? Can you distinguish between what it costs to acquire new users through advertising and promotions and what it costs to retain them by maintaining a data warehouse of purchases, frequency of use, and complaints?

- Can you predict the next three waves of market growth and the source of your own growth? When benchmarking competitors, do you look outside your current product categories? Do you know your share of your customers' overall spending—on food, for instance, or leisure activities?

- Are you actively searching for the next round of invention?

The keys to survival and prosperity are outside your window. Talk to consumers about their experiences. Ask the right questions to understand their dissatisfactions. Consumers are usually eager to supply even the most minute details if they think the information will help you make their lives easier and more exciting. Discovering the best solutions to consumers' problems requires time, energy, and skilled interactions.

There is an alternative to extinction. A company's vitality depends on fresh insights about consumers and competitors. It requires a sharp pencil and a clean sheet of paper to test "what ifs." It calls for courage and commitment. The next 40 years will deliver a new leading retailer and a new leading manufacturer. One of them could be you.

This article was first published in December 1998.

Exhibit 19

The Top 25 Worldwide Retailers in 1960

	1960 Revenues (in 1997 $millions)	1997 Revenues (in 1997 $millions)	1960–1997 Real CAGR[1]
Great Atlantic & Pacific Tea	27,426	10,262	–3%
Sears, Roebuck	21,604	41,296	2%
Safeway	12,902	22,484	1%
Kroger	9,773	26,567	3%
J.C. Penney	7,676	30,546	4%
Montgomery Ward	6,527	5,386[2]	–1%
F.W. Woolworth	5,410	6,624	1%
Edeka	5,344	32,654	5%
American Stores	5,286	19,139	3%
National Tea	4,472	acquired	NA
Federated Department Stores	4,105	15,668	4%
Food Fair Stores	4,030	acquired	NA
Winn-Dixie Stores	3,770	13,218	3%
May Department Stores	3,579	12,685	3%
Allied Stores	3,556	acquired	NA
Grand Union	3,158	2,266	–1%
First National Stores	2,803	acquired	NA
Jewel Tea	2,680	acquired	NA
W.T. Grant	2,679	bankrupt	NA
R.H. Macy	2,658	acquired	NA
Colonial Stores	2,328	acquired	NA
S.S. Kresge (Kmart)	2,185	32,183	7%
Gimbel Brothers	2,127	bankrupt	NA
Karstadt	1,663	15,306	6%
Kaufhof	1,579	acquired	NA

SOURCES: *Fortune,* Hoover's company profiles, annual reports, BCG estimates.

[1]Compound annual growth rate.

[2]Currently under Chapter 11 bankruptcy protection.

Exhibit 20

The Top 25 Worldwide Retailers in 1997

	1960 Revenues (in 1997 $millions)	1997 Revenues (in 1997 $millions)	1960–1997 Real CAGR[1]
Wal-Mart	did not exist	119,299	NA
Sears, Roebuck	21,604	41,296	2%
Metro	did not exist	37,212	NA
Rewe	1,308	35,355	9%
Edeka	5,344	32,654	5%
Intermarché-Spar AG	did not exist	32,394	NA
Kmart	2,185	32,183	7%
J.C. Penney	7,676	30,546	4%
Tengelmann	—	29,234	NA
Carrefour	7	29,000	25%
Dayton Hudson	549	27,757	11%
Kroger	9,773	26,567	3%
Leclerc	5	26,200	24%
Daiei	115	26,138	15%
Ahold	144	25,923	15%
Ito-Yokado	584	24,949	14%
Home Depot	did not exist	24,156	NA
Tesco	527	22,766	10%
Safeway	12,902	22,484	1%
J. Sainsbury	1,434	21,959	7%
Costco	did not exist	21,874	NA
Auchan	did not exist	20,567	NA
American Stores	5,286	19,139	3%
Promodès	371	18,966	11%
Aldi	200	18,606	13%

[1]Compound annual growth rate.

Exhibit 21

The Top 25 Worldwide Consumer-Goods Companies in 1960

	1960 Revenues (in 1997 $millions)	1997 Revenues (in 1997 $millions)	1960–1997 Real CAGR[1]
Unilever	20,112	51,611	3%
Nestlé	11,721	48,274	4%
Japan Tobacco	11,532	29,867	3%
National Dairy Products	8,712	acquired	NA
Procter & Gamble	7,533	35,764	4%
Distillers	5,693	acquired	NA
General Foods	5,681	acquired	NA
British-American Tobacco	5,136	24,005	4%
Borden	4,996	3,482	–1%
Kodak	4,937	14,713	3%
R.J. Reynolds Tobacco	4,159	17,057	4%
American Tobacco	3,784	3,551	0%
Seagram	3,557	12,560	3%
Canada Packers	3,120	acquired	NA
Colgate-Palmolive	3,012	9,057	3%
General Mills	2,810	5,609	2%
Kirin Brewery	2,750	12,438	4%
Campbell Soup	2,675	7,964	3%
Ralston Purina	2,666	4,487	1%
Coca-Cola	2,623	18,868	5%
National Biscuit	2,361	acquired	NA
American Home Products	2,333	5,850	2%
Beatrice Foods	2,315	acquired	NA
Standard Brands	2,315	acquired	NA
Continental Foods	2,220	19,734	6%

[1]Compound annual growth rate.

Exhibit 22

The Top 25 Worldwide Consumer-Goods Companies in 1997

	1960 Revenues (in 1997 $millions)	1997 Revenues (in 1997 $millions)	1960–1997 Real CAGR[1]
Philip Morris	1,727	56,114	10%
Unilever	20,112	51,611	3%
Nestlé	11,721	48,274	4%
Procter & Gamble	7,533	35,764	4%
Japan Tobacco	11,532	29,867	3%
Pepsico	824	29,292	10%
BAT Industries	5,136	24,005	4%
ConAgra	264	24,002	13%
Johnson & Johnson	1,578	22,629	7%
Diageo	—	20,305	NA
Sara Lee	2,220	19,734	6%
Coca-Cola	2,623	18,868	5%
RJR Nabisco	4,159	17,057	4%
Danone Group	684	15,164	8%
Mars	1,306	15,000	7%
Kodak	4,937	14,713	3%
Archer Daniels Midland	1,254	13,853	7%
IBP	172	13,259	12%
Seagram	3,557	12,560	4%
Kimberly-Clark	2,110	12,547	5%
Kirin Brewery	2,750	12,438	4%
L'Oréal	199	11,847	11%
Coca-Cola Enterprises	did not exist	11,278	NA
Anheuser-Busch	1,613	11,066	5%
Fuji Photo Film	661	10,346	8%

[1]Compound annual growth rate.

Michael S. Deimler and James M. Whitehurst

Whether they are manufacturers, retailers, or service providers, all consumer companies want and need to generate superior returns for share-holders. A growing number of companies understand that to maximize shareholder value, they must encourage their organizations to think like investors. But implanting that perspective in an organization can be difficult.

- Managers need to know what goals they're striving for; that means agreeing on how to measure value creation and on the appropriate target.

- They need to understand how various strategies translate into shareholder value.

- They need to encourage employees to do things differently by rewarding behavior that creates real economic value for shareholders.

Giving employees stock or options alone does not suffice. Internal performance measures tied to the creation of shareholder value are also extremely important. With that in mind, many executives are taking a new approach to running their businesses, which we call *shareholder value management*. SVM can be useful in many consumer services companies. Consider how it could be applied to an airline.

Choosing the Right Measures

Despite some improvement in recent years, airlines have been a high-risk, low-return investment, with total long-term returns to shareholders well below the stock market's average (see Exhibit 23). That shouldn't be surprising: on average, airlines' financial returns haven't even covered the cost of capital. As a result, airline executives are urgently searching for ways to make their business more attractive.

A critical first step is to install a suite of measures that enable the airline to see whether it has generated value for shareholders and how much more it is likely to create. The ultimate gauge of a company's success in creating value is, of course, total shareholder return (TSR), which is the appre-

Exhibit 23
Airlines Have Underperformed Relative to the Market

	1988–1998 Ten-Year Annualized TSR (%)
Alaska Air	8.7
AMR Corp.	8.3
Continental Airlines	18.9
Delta Air Lines	8.8
Southwest Airlines	27.8
UAL Corp.	12.2
U.S. Airways	4.3
Valueline Air Transport Industry	10.1
Market average	18.9

ciation (or depreciation) of the share price plus total dividends. TSR is a simple, objective measure for comparing the investment performances of companies.

What measures can help an executive predict the impact of a strategic decision on TSR? Traditional measures such as earnings per share (EPS) are usually poor predictors. Not only is EPS subject to accounting distortions that have little to do with the underlying cash flow generated by the company, but it also overlooks the level of investment made to achieve the returns. In other words, EPS fails to measure the cash invested (the asset base) against the cash generated (cash flow). EPS also neglects to relate an airline's return on investment to its cost of capital, which reveals the true value being created for shareholders.

No measure can give a complete picture of likely shareholder returns, but cash-based measures come much closer than traditional accounting-based measures (see Exhibit 24). Companies can use a broad range of cash measures to indicate whether value is being created for shareholders. (See Exhibit 25.)

Exhibit 24

Cash Measures Are a Better Predictor of Shareholder Value than EPS

Deviation of predicted stock price from actual price (%)

	EPS[1]	Cash measure[2]
AMR Corp.	52	5
Delta Air Lines	78	6
Southwest Airlines	24	9
UAL Corp.	71	9

NOTE: The time period is 1987 through 1997.

[1]Stock price predicted using a constant multiple of EPS.

[2]Capitalized cash value added.

Making Strategic Choices

Perhaps the most important benefit of SVM is that it can help managers evaluate a broad range of strategic options. Take, for example, the question of growth. How much growth is best, and should an airline ever grow at the expense of profitability? By measuring the effect of growth on shareholder value, SVM makes explicit the tradeoffs between asset growth and profitability. Because investors reward both, improvement in one dimension may offset a conscious, strategic decline in the other. Lacking tools to make such tradeoffs, some airlines have overlooked valuable opportunities for growth.

Consider another common strategic decision: where to deploy assets, which for airlines means selecting the optimal network of routes to fly. Currently, most airlines generally evaluate routes on the basis of traditional measures such as operating margin and revenue per available seat mile (RASM). But measuring performance on the basis of operating margin and RASM, without considering the differences in aircraft investments across routes, may produce wildly inaccurate views of performance and lead to the suboptimal allocation of aircraft.

For example, airlines sometimes cancel or decide not to fly routes that are a drag on the average margin. But adding certain routes may improve overall return on investment by increasing asset utilization: an airline can increase the time that its fleet is in the air, thereby making more capacity available for sale without any additional investment. However, if an airline adds flights at 2 a.m., when there is little demand, asset utilization may increase but ROI may not. Using measures of asset productivity and cash-based ROI would help airlines allocate assets to routes that would generate the highest shareholder returns.

Airlines must also make complex investment decisions about assets other than aircraft. Such assets represent a large portion of an airline's total investment. Once approved and on the books, however, these assets are often all but forgotten. Maintenance departments, for instance, generally prefer to have a buffer inventory of important spares, and because parts are a balance-sheet item, they don't affect anyone's cost budget. Yet holding inventory does have a real cost—a capital cost. Only when the cost of holding such assets is included in assessments of maintenance performance can an airline set optimal inventory levels.

Raising performance in one dimension can sometimes lower it overall. The trick for airlines, as for many other businesses, is to optimize a series of complex tradeoffs. The SVM approach allows companies to predict how these interdependent tradeoffs would affect shareholder value.

Creating a Common Language

Companies can also incorporate an SVM approach into their management and board reports. Over time, the increasing use of SVM measures will create a common language for managers, board members, and the investment community. With a rigorous framework that everyone understands, managers can explain the impact of their decisions in terms of shareholder value to one another, to employees, and ultimately to investors and analysts. The SVM framework is applicable to many kinds of consumer marketing businesses. In addition to airlines, we have applied it successfully to the retail, packaged goods, and durables industries, and to various service industries.

Do *You* Need SVM?

Many consumer companies have yet to realize the benefits that an SVM approach can yield. Others have adopted SVM but have not tapped its full potential. Here are five questions to help senior executives test their need for SVM:

1. Have you de-averaged the economics of your company to determine which products and business units are creating value?

2. Are you making the right tradeoffs between growth and profitability?

3. Do you have cash-based measures that accurately reveal the creation of shareholder value?

4. Do you reward people on the basis of the value they create for shareholders?

5. Do you know which strategic tradeoffs would generate the performance required to double your stock price in four years? And do you know what actions this requires from each of your managers?

Shareholders are tough taskmasters. They expect straight answers to questions like the ones above. But they will reward the companies that come closest to getting the answers right.

A version of this article, titled "Building Shareholder Value," appeared in the February 1999 issue of *Airline Business.*

This article was first published in June 1999.

Exhibit 25

Guide to Cash-Based Measures

Operating cash flow (OCF) measures the amount of cash flow that business operations generate. Although a useful starting point, OCF does not take into account the cash investment required to generate returns.

Cash flow return on investment (CFROI) measures the efficiency of a business in producing cash flow returns in relation to the gross cash invested to earn the returns. CFROI can also be compared with the cost of capital to determine whether a business is creating or destroying value.

Cash value added (CVA) measures the return generated by the business minus a charge for the capital used in generating the returns. CVA can also be interpreted as the spread between CFROI and the cost of capital, multiplied by the asset base. A business with a positive value added is generating returns above the cost of capital. This is a particularly good measure for businesses that require a disciplined approach to the cost and efficiency of their asset bases.

Equity free cash flow (FCF) measures the net amount of cash that a business generates for equity holders. FCF differs from OCF because changes in the capital required to run the business and financing impacts are netted out against OCF.

Total business return (TBR) models the total shareholder return that common investors receive from equity ownership by incorporating the expected change in share price plus any dividend payout (FCF). Several cash-flow methodologies exist for calculating the expected change in equity value. TBR is the most comprehensive and accurate measure of value creation because it incorporates both the immediate impact of the free cash flow (the dividend) and the capitalized value of change in returns and growth (the share price appreciation).

Note: Operating leases must be capitalized for calculating CFROI, CVA, and OCF.

Michael J. Silverstein

In this last Opportunity for Action of 1999, we present six challenges. Pursuing them with force, resolve, and skill will enable your company to  achieve breakthrough success. It will require rising to a new level of aspiration and courage. Master these challenges and you will become a domain expert capable of achieving market light speed.

1. Immerse Yourself in Your Domain

Pablo Picasso is the classic example of a domain expert. He began his artistic life when he was only five, completing his father's paintings. His family used its savings to send him to classical art school, where he was quickly recognized as a prodigy for his ability to capture light, color, and line. Having mastered the rules, he was then ready to challenge their hegemony. Eventually he transcended the old formulas by transforming them into his own aesthetic, which was simplified, stylized, and exaggerated. The master student of Velázquez and Monet reinvented art with his interpretations of form and materials. His productivity was founded on experience, repetition, ambition, and raw talent.

Domain expertise *demands* total immersion in the art and science of your endeavor. Like Picasso, you must know how and why things work—today as well as yesterday—before you can use your own personal vision and energy to create new ways of working. Picasso immersed himself in the art of the past, then added his own personal vision and energy to establish himself as an original.

2. Experience Your Brand

Few manufacturers and retailers experience their offerings the way consumers do. Experience Your Brand (EYB) is our methodology for learning how consumers become aware of products and services, how they experience the purchasing process, how they respond to the product or service, and how likely they are to become loyal customers. Applying the lessons of industrial engineering, EYB helps marketers view consumers in an economic framework. It takes into account the cost of acquiring customers, the value gained from particular purchases, the investment needed to nurture and cement relationships, and the options for connecting with and delivering to various segments.

Employing EYB—which requires senior managers to shop with consumers and visit them in their homes—can be electrifying. For example, we recently accompanied the CEO of a packaged goods company on a visit to "Joan"—a 38-year-old mother of four who feeds her family on $57 a week. For the CEO, who had been reluctant to come along, it was an eye-opening experience. To his surprise, he found that Joan stored his product in the back of her pantry and used it only sporadically, "when I remember it's there." After learning in subsequent interviews with consumers that Joan was hardly the exception, the CEO vowed to change his brand's package, labels, usage directions, advertising, and quality. He also switched from investing in market research—which invariably ended up buried in unread tomes— to engaging in frequent interactions with individual consumers.

EYB involves observing consumers directly, adjusting product specifications, and continuously improving. It requires a maniacal attention to detail. From such detail you will generate a stream of refinements that can catapult you to the next level of success.

Ask yourself these questions:

- Do I have a map of the consumer's experience?

- Do I know the points of defection?

- Do I know the net present value of a household that uses my products and the leverage points for increasing frequency, longevity, and loyalty?

- Am I using my discretionary investment to manage the mix between old, broad-market promotional advertising and new tools, such as personal communication, sales-force enhancement, frontline data collection, and dissatisfaction discovery?

3. Invent to Drive Advantage

You must be ahead of the market to anticipate shifts and improve your position with successful innovations. Our research across all categories indicates that sustained improvement in market share occurs only as a result of new product introductions. Higher levels of advertising and promotion rarely produce long-term share gains. Today's sophisticated consumers gravitate to product improvements, new applications, and breakthroughs that offer variety and value, and save time. Deliver innovations like these and your customers will become brand apostles who will be much more effective than paid commercials in persuading others to buy your products. Word-of-mouth recommendation is the most frequently cited reason for trying a new product or service. Recommendations are driven by inventions.

4. Sell Dreams, Not Reality

People can be logical, intelligent, and thoughtful, but they can also be emotional, passionate, moody, impulsive, inflexible, and in search of instant gratification. Consumers buy what they dream about, not necessarily what they *need.* Few Western consumers lack clothes, shoes, or stereos. You have to make them want more of these things. You must romance them into desiring what you have to offer. It's all about fashion and excitement. Appeal to their emotions and memories. Satisfied dreams justify price premiums. Functional excellence is usually just a table stake.

5. Create a Values Legacy

Wal-Mart ends this century at the pinnacle of success. You can be the Sam Walton of your market by creating a value-based business model. The beauty of Wal-Mart is its simplicity—the proposition is crystal clear to all associates and consumers.

"We'll lower the cost of living for everyone," Walton proclaimed. He used limited advertising, relying on word-of-mouth recommendations to bring people to his stores. He relentlessly studied every line item to reduce costs, increase value, and make the Wal-Mart brand more visible to consumers. He believed in "Buy 'em low, stack 'em high, and sell 'em cheap." He created a share-value growth machine driven by expansion, low cost, and high returns.

Walton transformed his stores from the old five-and-dime format to broadline carriers of apparel, home textiles, garden tools, sporting goods, toys, music, and more. Then he moved into food and financial services. He used each new location to test and experiment, rapidly rolling out his winning ideas. He managed each store as a separate competitive zone with information-empowered resident managers. Eventually he used cash from one location to fund the next. And finally, he applied an acquisition formula that allowed him to exploit his advantage. It involved revamping old stores and repricing and rebadging old products—all to serve the customer better. International growth was locally derived. Wal-Mart took its format to CIFRA in Mexico and Wertkauf in Germany. It did the same in the U.K., where today Wal-Mart is integrating ASDA into its family.

Walton's miracle of retailing uses cost advantage as its competitive hammer—60 basis points in distribution, 410 basis points in store operations, 160 basis points in corporate overhead. The business system translates into lower inventory, fewer out-of-stocks, and reduced distribution costs. It is powered by the world's largest commercial database—at 24 terabytes, it is larger than the database of the Library of Congress. This wealth of information makes for better micromerchandising, sales planning, labor scheduling, and innovation rollouts.

Seven years after Walton's death, Wal-Mart's culture is still steeped in his formula for success. The values live on. Take the lessons of Wal-Mart—simplicity, value, reproducibility—and apply them to your own enterprise.

6. Leverage the Power of the Web

Consumers, who control most of the world's wealth, have become increasingly proficient at using the Web. That revolution has made communication nearly free. It means that you can—and *must*—reach out to and interact with every consumer in every demographic segment. You can learn how to use the Web to inspire consumers. You can use it to deliver a flawless experience. Personalized communication on the Web keeps people coming back. If you use your relationship and knowledge base, you can take your best customers to a new level of activity. They are your most precious and leverageable asset.

The next consumer-marketing revolution will bring broadband communication into people's homes, enabling companies to forge intimate and loyal relationships and to respond instantly to consumers' needs and desires. The Web has shifted from being a toy to being a tool. Now is the time to learn about electronic purchasing behavior and brand adoption, and to master the new rules of marketing, by which the attentive know their customers intimately.

*   *   *

We are passionate about breakthrough insight. These six challenges can be the seeds of a transformation. But to tap their potential, you must be open to insights and new ideas.

As you begin the year 2000, set out to capture consumers' imaginations. Break through the status quo. Don't believe it when they tell you it can't be done. Let your dreams inspire a new reality.

This article was first published in December 1999.

Breaking Compromises

ক

Designed by Carter Halliday Associates

Illustrations by James Steinberg

Index